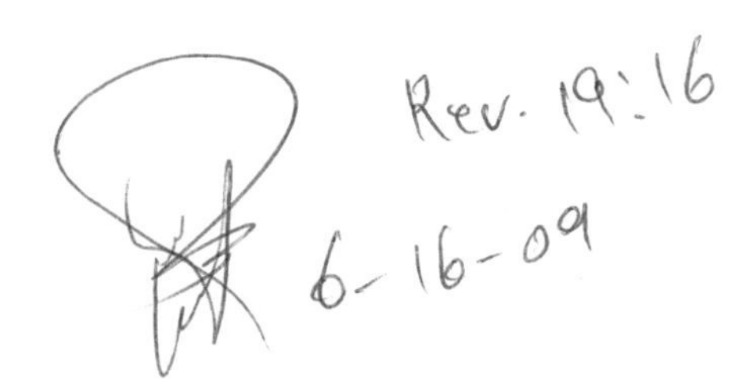

Christ Above All Gods

In Whom Will You Trust?

Dr. Daniel SHAYESTEH
Author

Christ above all gods

Requests for information should be addressed to the author:

PO Box 1885, New Castle, NSW 1765 Australia

ISBN: 0-9756017-0-9

Cover Design: Janet Shayesteh

Published by Daniel Shayesteh

Contents

Preface

Most people do not know that the major problems in the world have arisen out of the worship of false gods. These false gods have revealed themselves as the producers and inspirers of every evil thought, word and deed in their so-called sacred books. Their dualistic nature, in turn, is instilled amongst the community, making it impossible for people to establish peace within their family, society or the world. Indeed people are not able to respect the rights of others, unless they come out of the bondage of these unreliable gods. Believing in dualistic gods, who are not able to solve the problem of evil, is nothing different to sanctioning an invasion that tears down the peace within a family and the world community.

Therefore, the purpose of this book is to challenge the hearts, minds and consciences of all who read it that they might discover the only true and holy One, who is the source of purity, oneness and unity. This is the One who can rid the nations of dualism, disunity and division.

Impure and dualistic gods are the cause of divisions, disunity and hostility. If God is not pure and has division within His own nature, He will in no way be able to lead people to peace with one another, even though they may long for unity and peace in their inner being. For this reason, this book aims to draw people's attention to the deeper layers of religions, and to distinguish the true religion from the false.

There are many religions in the world and also extreme variations within each religion as a result of constant interference throughout history. Covering all religions and their sects was not the mission of this book. The overriding focus of this book is on the differences amongst gods and their stands against Satan or Evil. Except in Christianity, gods in most other religions more or less hold a similar stand towards Satan. By evaluating the main religions, I have indirectly evaluated almost all the world's religions. I also thought it would be better to give a very brief introduction about each religion to encourage and help the readers to undertake further studies.

I pray that this book may become a blessed tool for many who have not had the opportunity to evaluate the deeper layers of their beliefs and who were not aware of how their own individual life and their families and their societies could be invaded by false gods and religions.

I also take this opportunity to voice my appreciation to all those who encouraged me to write this book and who helped me to bring this book to its present stage. However, they have not played a role in formulating any part of the arguments and conclusions I have made throughout the book and therefore I take full responsibility for what is written.

Daniel Shayesteh
January 2003

Introduction

Why Would People Follow a Religion?

Different reasons can be traced for the interest of people in one religion over another. Often at times, it is not their interest, but the external forces imposed on people, that leave them no choice but to follow a particular religion. For example, whenever people are unable to control their surrounding human or natural forces, they prefer to show allegiance rather than be killed. The same applies when people are compelled to follow a certain religion.

People also believe that the Creator of the universe is the highest authority and desires everybody to be under His control and in harmony with Him. This is another reason why people follow the religion practiced by their community in order to try and fulfill the desires of their Creator.

The development of civilization has also led some people to search for an explanation that provides purpose, goals and hope for their lives and life itself. This has led them to select an idea or religion that best meets their needs in order to attain their goals.

Why Understand Religions?

Willingly or unwillingly, every person in the world is affected by religion. Various ethnicities hold religious values that mean they act or react differently to other people, at least in some areas of their beliefs. There are differences everywhere, and the differences are reflected in the society and in everybody's relationship and fellowship with others. Even atheists have not been able to remove religious values from their lives. Therefore, religious values are present everywhere we go. They are present in the lives of everybody with whom we have contact, as we share the opportunities provided by living in a society, small or large. Therefore, understanding each other's beliefs is of vital importance for the well being of a society. It helps us to discover the long lasting values for establishing unceasing relationship and friendship with one another. Ignorance, indifference and passive tolerance, that always accompany lack of understanding, enhance miscommunication and alienation and therefore can create catastrophic events in the community, such as happened on September 11th - heartbreaking and irreparable forever. There are ample examples of various communities that have lived in a country side by side for centuries and in some cases for thousands of years, but are still alien or hostile to each other. The main reason for this is misunderstanding or lack of understanding.

Another influence we see today is how, unavoidably, the internationalization of technology (globalization) has brought people of various nations together and forced almost all countries in the world to taste multiculturalism, a blessing in many ways. However, the curse arises where people do not understand each other and are not integrated peacefully.

Secularism was not able to provide people with a proper understanding of multiculturalism. It welcomed people from all cultural and religious backgrounds, but ignored the great need to discover the deeper cultural or religious tastes that was carried by each person when they traveled to new places. All that we have inherited from secularism is a 'passive' approach to tolerance in which people are no longer able to question the changes that have occurred in society. Passive tolerance is not like creative tolerance that promotes knowledge and search for the best. Instead, it is an ignorant and indifferent tolerance that can be as harmful as aggression.

Many believed that through the advancement of technology, together with sovereign social laws, the authorities would be able to create a friendlier atmosphere and lead their multi-ethnic societies towards unification. But they neglected the huge effect of religion and therefore overlooked the fact that people respect their religious beliefs more than they do the law of the society. Some religious people believe that, in some cases, they have to break the law for the sake of religious vows. Clearly, religion has a deep root in people's ethical, moral, political, economic and social values. It has to be understood deeply.

People tend to only look at the external layers of religious messages and then proclaim them all to be the same and heading towards the same goal. Very few in the world have looked at the deeper layers of the religions and analyzed the nature of the various gods in order to see whether or not they are the same. That is why any time religious conflicts arise among different groups, many shake their heads and say, 'They head toward the same goal; we don't know why they are against each other'. Unfortunately very few have made an scholarly study in order to realize the differences. Time and time again we hear some say, 'Well, it's the different interpretations of their religion which have led them to this stage or to acts of terrorism'. It is true that to some degree the different interpretations affect people's relationship with one another, but the major problem of the world is ignorance and lack of understanding by individuals.

People are not normally encouraged or interested in spending any time evaluating the motivations that 'lie behind the scenes' and that have major effects in the long run. Leaders in various countries have been successful when they took advantage of this public ignorance. This has enabled them to portray themselves as lovers of people and keepers of peace and justice whilst at the same time slyly fulfilling their selfish desires. Even more influential were those who flavored their dictatorship with religious values enabling them to trap ignorant people in the claws of their inhuman desires.

Since gods and religions dominate the lives of many in the world, followers must wake up and evaluate the ability of their belief system to positively contribute to their own life, society and the world.

Any guru or "divine being" who has said, 'Do not lie, do not steal, be not wicked, do not kill' and so on, must be analyzed to see if their lives are transparent and in perfect unity with their messages. People, who are following a god, need to become certain that he has a pure nature and not a dualistic one (having both light and darkness) which cannot match with honesty, love, peace and justice. A dualistic god is a problem as his message consists of two opposing forces. The life he builds is dualistic, the goal for life he gives is dualistic and the righteousness and peace that he calls for are dualistic. When he enters one's life, he cannot plant purity and oneness in the heart, but only a mixture of love and hatred, a mixture of success and failure, and so on. His inconsistent nature results in 'double standard' lives. He cannot survive on love alone, but also needs deceit, force, hatred, hostility, ignorance or bigotry. His dualistic nature leads people to blind obedience and thereby he becomes the unquestionable god of all generations. Not even the mighty forces or laws of the super-power countries can rid his hostile values from the heart and mind of his followers. Many times we have seen the leaders of the world, despite the greatness of their political powers, afraid of the hostile spirit of the false gods who run the life of the majority. Fear has prevented them from condemning the spirit of a religion that holds a society to ransom. Furthermore, in some cases, they even praised the spirit placing the blame for the repressed societies on the men and women who were the agents of the evil spirit. Instead of cutting the evil at its root, they only chipped away at the branches. After a while, many more branches grew from where each branch had been pruned, and not only were nations unable to live a peaceful life, but also fell under the threat of many bloodthirsty and unsociable rebellious leaders. Nothing other than "knowledge and understanding" could rescue nations from this threat. As the Bible states;

> *When a country is rebellious, it has many rulers, but a man of understanding and knowledge maintains order* (Prov.28:2).

Religious problems cannot be solved through political pressure and games or through the authority of social laws. This is because in the heart of people, religion supercedes all other aspects of life. The only solution for religious problems is to work at the level of people's hearts, minds and consciences. People need encouragement and help to evaluate and broaden their understanding, leading them to select the best and most genuine religion. This process of evaluation is costly in some countries, resulting in the death penalty for those who undertake such a course. However, freedoms in other countries provide a golden opportunity for many to investigate the foundation of religions. People in these countries have the freedom to choose the best religion and are able to carry out evangelism and mission to those people who have been deprived of this freedom in other lands.

The Basis for Bringing about a Change in the Quality of People's Lives

Knowledge and information opens the eyes of people and unites them to improve the quality of their physical and spiritual lives. On the contrary ignorance pushes people apart and leads them towards extreme narrow-mindedness and degrades the quality of their life. The quality of religious life improves when someone chooses to be open-minded, but narrow-minded religious people excommunicate themselves from the beauty of life. A beautiful life and its author cannot be discovered through a static mind. It is a shame for the author of life to have blind followers. Look what the God of Israel said to her even though she was honoring Him with the best of her wealth;

> *For the Lord has spoken: "I reared children and brought them up, but they have rebelled against me. The ox knows his master, the donkey his owner's manger, but Israel does not know, my people do not understand...I have no pleasure in the blood of bulls and lambs and goats...Stop bringing meaningless offerings. Your incense is detestable to me...Come now let us reason together* (Isa. 1:2-3, 11c, 13a, 18a).

> *Who is blind but my servant, and deaf like the messenger I send? Who is blind like the one committed to me, blind like the servant of the LORD? You have seen many things, but have paid no attention; your ears are*

> *open, but you hear nothing. It pleased the Lord for the sake of his righteousness to make his law great and glorious*" (Isa. 42: 19-21).

God had no pleasure in their sacrifices while they continued to close their eyes to a deeper understanding. A belief must not be blindly accepted nor in the same way be rejected or left behind without reasoning. We are the creatures of insight, reason and logic; leaving a religion and accepting the other without an understanding of the tenets of each is like being blind and deaf. Can we win any favor with God by our lack of understanding?

Research and investigation are beneficial in any situation. It will help the world to rescue itself from the crisis of false religions and ideas and lead its nations to unity and oneness. Look at how open-minded Jesus was; look at the Bible's call for openness, searching, comparison and decision making;

> *Does not the ear test words as the tongue tastes food?* (Job 12:11; 34:3)

> *Choose...knowledge rather than choice gold...I have understanding and power* (Prov.8:10,14).

"You will seek me and find me when you seek me with all your heart. I will be found", declares the LORD (Jer. 29: 13-14).

Jesus said, "You will know the truth, and the truth will set you free (John 8:32).

Test everything, hold on to the good. Avoid every kind of evil (1Thes. 5:21-22).

You may say to yourselves, "How can we know when a message has not been spoken by the LORD?" If what a prophet claims in the name of the LORD does not take place or come true, that is a message the LORD has not spoken. That prophet has spoken presumptuously. Do not be afraid of him (Deut. 18:21-22).

You have let go of the command of God and are holding on to the traditions of men (Mark 7:8). *Your faith might not rest on men's wisdom, but on God's power* (1Cor. 2:5).

See to it that no one takes you captive through hollow and deceptive philosophy, which depends on human tradition and the basic principles of this world rather than on Christ (Col.2:8).

He will punish those who do not know God...They will be punished with everlasting

> *destruction and shut out from the presence of the Lord and from the majesty of his power on the day he comes to be glorified in his holy people and to be marveled at among all those who have believed* (2Thes.1:9-10b).

> *Although they* (men) *claimed to be wise, they became fools and exchanged the glory of the immortal God for images made to look like mortal man and birds and animals and reptiles* (Rom. 1:22-23).

> *My purpose is that they may be encouraged in heart and united in love, so that they may have the full riches of complete understanding, in order that they may know the mystery of God, namely, Christ, in whom are hidden all the treasures of wisdom and knowledge* (Col.2:2).

> *Formerly, when you did not know God, you were slaves to those who by nature are not gods. But now... you know God* (Gal. 4:8-9).

No other religion in the world has encouraged such a deep understanding of what is needed for the exodus from ignorance and blind obedience.

Our contemporary era is the era of a boom in education. It should be the era where people seek the answers to the most difficult questions of life. The need to search for the best religion is more urgent than ever since the rise of man.

Internationalization and Globalization have taken their giant steps across national borders, ignoring the barriers that exist amongst the nations and bringing them much closer to each other. Globalization needs to stretch its hands to the deeper levels of the cultural and religious values of the nations in order to find the best values for better integration of the world. The omnipresent and omniscient Spirit of Christ supports this contemporary research. Jesus claimed that He was the Lord of all time (Matt. 28:18-20; Heb. 13:8). He certainly is pleased with those who have a bigger picture for life and for the world. He knows that if we do not have a full understanding of the world's values, we will be easily influenced by the ideas and beliefs that have always tried to impose themselves forcefully on societies. People need to have intellectual reasons for anything and anybody they choose to follow.

Some Tips About a Genuine Religion or Belief

1. The true belief or religion must be able to plant the Spirit of the Real God in the heart and life of people in a practical sense and drive out the evil spirit.

2. True religion must respect the free will of any individual in the world.

3. True religion does not impose itself on others, but instead respects the voice of free will and becomes open to world-wide criticism.

4. True religion does not compromise by working with ulterior motives, but encourages honesty, as the essential quality required in human relationships.

5. True religion comes to serve humankind by becoming a tool for the development of a warm and wide understanding among diverse nations in order to remove the barriers to unity among them.

6. True religion allows people to scrutinize its values and its leader's life in order to learn more about and have a deeper understanding of the concepts and ideas that are the basis of that religion.

7. True religion calls upon people to refer to their own God given capability, examine the words of prophets and religious leaders, search for the best possible values in the world and choose the best with a free will. The truth cannot be discovered by blindly following or obeying the guidance of someone who has never been open to comparison and has never allowed others to do it.

8. A true religion overcomes the spiritual uncertainty many feel in this world and gives certainty for the future.

9. A true religion meets the 'at all times' criteria of truthfulness, and becomes the good example for all generations.

Everybody Is God in Hinduism

Background
India is the place of Hinduism's origin and development. The earliest worship in Hinduism was animistic. Hinduism was not founded on the teaching of anyone and has reached to its present state under the influence of many nations, cultures, beliefs and practices. External factors have turned it into a 'store room' of ideas, beliefs and traditions, making it hard to derive a sound doctrine. Some people believe in one god while some others believe in many and some in none; some follow a life of privation and meditation while some others follow a completely opposite route, taking part in a sexual cult; while some are tolerant, others are ruthless and harsh. In this way, the values contradict each other sharply.

There is no false religion for Hinduism; all religions are good, have the same goal and lead to the same god. This is because men and women of every faith are considered the manifestations of the same Supreme Being, having the same goal and destination.

Some Hindu teachers regard Jesus as divine Lord and His words the same in essence with the words of their scriptures.

Hindus also worship demonic spirits, the living saints, animals such as cows, monkeys, snakes and others. This does not mean that every god is eternal. Some of them are the offspring of others and like all things they also will pass away. Gods exercise their power in favor of or in opposition to men and women, depending on their respectful or disrespectful deeds towards those gods. Sometimes gods merge into one because they are the manifestations of the same supreme reality that desires the ultimate oneness of all that exists. However, the issue of how inferior gods, who have personalities that merge with one another, can be absorbed into the ultimate god, who has no personality, is an issue that brings the authenticity of Hindu philosophy under question.

It is believed that sometimes a deity allows himself to be born on the earth in order to conquer evil and restore peace and order. An incarnation of a god is called an *avatar*.

Hindus believe the whole universe and every thing that exists, including gods, are subject to constant change; nothing is permanent. Mountains and rocks will disappear, even the gods will pass away and others will take their places. For Hindus, each soul has many lives that die and are reborn again and again.

Nature of God and the Effect

Some Hindus take gods as separate and distinct divine beings whereas others think of them as different ways of looking at the one reality. The following divisions give a brief description of the nature of Hindu gods and their effect on creation:

1. *Henotheism* (ancient Vedas[1] and later Vishnavism and Shivaism[2]) states that many gods exist, but the supreme reality is one. It is Brahman, the eternal power who controls the universe and is more important than the others. Brahman is made up of many divinities. The three most important ones are:

- *Brahma*, who is the creator of the universe. The lifetime of Brahma is 12000 divine years, which is equivalent to 4,320,000 human years. The universe endures as long as the god lives. Brahma is married and his wife is called Sarasvati.

- *Vishnu*, who helps the creator in building the universe and in battle against the enemy. Any time the need arises, Vishnu appears in various living forms (such as a fish or tortoise or boar or dwarf or Buddha, etc.), in order to deliver a person or the world from the power of evil.

---

[1] *Veda* means "divine knowledge, sacred lore, sacred books" and applies to the most ancient sacred literature of the Hindus (1500-1000 B.C.). There are four *Vedas*, which are the collections of psalms and hymns of praise, rule and rituals, and philosophy mixed with magic, which all together make up the Hindus' holy book. Aryans believed *Vedas* were given out to certain men whom the gods considered worthy to interpret it to people on earth.

[2] Vishnavism is the worship of Vishnu, and Shivaism is the worship of Shiva.

- *Shiva* (Siva), who is the destroyer often accompanied by evil spirits. One of the most important Hindu divinities is Shiva's wife, Shakti, who is famous for her two extreme dualistic natures;

    - The beloved and attractive goddess of motherhood, protection, healing and benevolence; in this form she is called *Parvati* or *Uma.*
    - The feared goddess of destruction, murder and savagery who personifies death and darkness; in this form she is called *Durga* or *Kali.*

These contrasting natures of the goddess describe birth, death and destruction in the reincarnation circle.

The destructing spirit of *Kali* is still in work in India. In the year 2002, Indian police recorded at least one human sacrifice a month through ritual killings in the name of *Kali.*[3]

Henotheism believes in the pre-existence of a primordial impersonal reality (the One) that manifests itself into multiple gods and creatures and is the origin of all.

There is a great philosophical mistake in the heart of this belief. Personal beings cannot become

---

[3] Time, July 29, 2002, Page 30.

impersonal, and an impersonal being also cannot manifest itself as personal beings. Since Brahman is believed to be impersonal and has no personality to be described, it then cannot manifest itself into other describable beings. Secondly, a complete being cannot multiply into inferior incomplete and opposite beings. This belief also shows that the evil (*Shiva*) is in Brahman and sin flows down from Brahman into other inferior forms.

2. *Pantheism*[4] (Upanishads[5] later called Vedanta) describes the one Supreme Being as an immaterial, impersonal, uncreated, transcendent, infinite, indescribable being that is the origin of all manifestations. It (Brahman) is the cause and reason for all that is. It desired to be multiplied and be born in many, and it said and became many.

The Upanishads teach that Brahman was born in every body, and the soul in every body is identical with Brahman. From this idea it follows that the more you meditate and understand yourself, the more likely you are to understand Brahman. This is why meditation has become so important in Hindu beliefs.

---

[4] *Pantheon* means god is everything, and everything is god, so that god and the world are of the same substance, though the form is different.

[5] *Upanishad* means 'sittings with a teacher'. Upanishads are the scriptures in dialogue or seminar form between pupil and teacher. These sacred writings were later called *Vedanta*.

Brahman has two distinct aspects. One aspect is absolute, which is transcendent, unmanifested, incomprehensible and inconceivable. However, the second aspect is relative, indwells everything and manifests itself as a describable being. All the products of its relative aspects - gods, humans, animals and matters - tend to return to the absolute one, evolving from one level of manifestation to another and ultimately become merged or absorbed into the impersonal aspect of the transcendent Brahman.

It is obvious that the same criticisms in *Henotheism* apply to *Pantheism* too. The return of the personal creature into the impersonal is something that does not make sense. If the return of the personal creatures of Brahman's relative nature to its impersonal nature was possible, the coming out or manifestation from absolute impersonal nature would also have been possible and therefore Brahman would not need a personal or relative aspect for manifestation and multiplication. In other words, if return and absorption of inferiors to the absolute was possible, departing from the absolute would also be possible. However, we know that it is impossible for the absolute impersonal god to manifest itself in other forms or absorb other beings into itself.

3. *Theism* sees god (Krishna) as a supreme personal god who is the cause and power behind all things in the world. He has attributes and therefore, he cannot be impersonal; he influences man by his

initiatives. He is the creator and the substance of the universe, either spiritual or material. Krishna too desires the evolution of all that exist into the supreme reality through the continual cycle of transformation.

Krishna is the revelation of the god Vishnu in his human form and has become the most popular of all Hindu deities. Alexander's invasion of India also brought with it ideas that rejected the idea of a god who is impersonal, but at the same time loves; an impersonal god cannot love. Therefore, a new religious trend appeared that at the end resulted in the birth of a baby god *Krishna* as the personal and loving god. After he grew to manhood, he danced and slept with women. The women's hunger for him is interpreted as every soul's longing for God.

4. *Shamkhya* and the *Yoga of Patanjali* admit two ultimate realities: *Purusha (equivalent to atman*[6]*)* and *Prakriti* (the primordial substance). *Purusha* is a universal impersonal soul that pervades all things and was never involved in the law of karma. *Prakriti* though is impersonal, but is capable of manifestation and is involved in the law of karma.

Prakriti has three inner material tendencies, called *gunas*:

- *Satva,* is the tendency that brings light, purity and knowledge;

---

[6] The word *atman* means '*individual soul'*, which is identical with the ultimate reality (Brahman) that controls all things from within.

- *Raias,* is responsible for activity, energy and dynamism;

- *Tamas,* opposes action, producing darkness, heaviness and ignorance.

One opposite inner primordial substance of god always tends to dominate the other. However, the *gunas* clashed against each other and the world came into being by the participation of a certain proportion of each of the three *gunas*.

The major problem of this belief is dualism, the existence of two ultimate realities. This will be described in the later section on Zoroastrianism. In this belief also, god is the creator of sin or darkness.

5. *Tantrism* and *Hatha Yoga* believe that the ultimate reality of the universe is the god Shiva. Shiva with his divine wife, Shakti, formed a state of primordial unity and unmanifestation. Shiva represents purity and transcendence, and Shakti, on the contrary, represents immanence and dynamism that opens the way for manifestation. The whole world came into existence as the result of a disunity and division between Shiva and Shakti who were once united.

The problem of this belief is that unmanifestation cannot be formed nor can it be divisible. In this belief also god is the cause of the spirit of rebellion, disunity and war in all that exists.

The idea of becoming merged or absorbed into the supreme reality (Brahman) lies behind all Hindu thought. Brahman is universal and impersonal and pervades all things, and all things that exist, exist in Brahman. Since Brahman pervades the atman (soul), therefore, Brahman and atman become identical and indistinguishable. The Hindu in this way concludes that atman and Brahman are one and the same. They are just different words that express the same idea. As a result, every Hindu can say, 'I am Brahman' or 'I have come face to face with a god'.

Literature

The oldest Hindu literatures are from the centuries between 1500 and 800 B.C. and are called *Vedict literature*. It contains mostly myths, stories about Hindu gods and goddesses and heroes, hymns (Rig-Veda), sacrificial rituals and a little doctrine.

Modern Hinduism has little to do with the ancient literature, because of the gradual additions and changes throughout the history of Hinduism.

Reincarnation

Hindus believe when a person or animal dies, only the physical body dies, the soul does not die but is reborn. This continuous process of rebirth is called reincarnation. In Hinduism animals like human beings have souls, and in reincarnation these souls evolve into human beings or decline from human beings into animals.

Karma

Literally, Karma means 'deed' or 'act'. Karma speaks about how the future life of a person in the next reincarnation is affected by his present thoughts and actions. No one can escape the consequence of his action in the life after reincarnation. Good deeds will lead his soul to be born into a saint or a higher state in the society but evil deeds will lead his soul to be born into a lower state, even into the body of a worm. The reincarnation continues until a person achieves an irreversible spiritual perfection of divinity. But the unsuccessful souls wander through many incarnations before reaching a state of divinity (salvation).

Yoga

Yoga means 'yoke' or 'path'. As a yoke disciplines an ox to walk a right path, so a yoga disciplines people to take control of their mind and body through asceticism, physical exercises, breathing techniques and meditation each depending on various schools of Yoga. Yoga is done to lead man to deification, helping man to discover the divine power within him and bringing him to unity with his internal divine power (god-self or Brahman). The exercise of Yoga breaks the limitations of people's minds and bodies and helps them to reach to the highest personal happiness in spite of outward difficulties. Hindus believe man is the extension of the divine being and can apply his godly power to his daily life by concentrating, not on the passing unreal world, but on the eternal and real, Brahman. In this way, he will be able to release the divinity within himself and rise above materialism and reach towards love and peace.

Questions & Answers

1. *What is God (Ultimate Reality) in Hinduism?*

God in Hinduism is an absolute as well as a relative being. As an absolute being, it ('it' in Hinduism) is one, pre-existent, impersonal, unmanifested and indescribable. As a relative being, it is manifested and multiplied into all that exists.

2. *What is the goal of Hinduism?*

The goal of Hinduism is to quit the world of impermanence and change and to be absorbed into the one permanent and unchanging reality (God).

3. *How do Hindus see the world?*

They see the world less than real, existing as the play of gods, almost an illusion.

4. *Why was the world created?*

The creation in Hinduism, unlike Christianity, is not because God was happy to create and therefore He desired and created. Instead, the disagreements within the nature of the Hindu god (i.e., amongst the inferior gods that make up the supreme god) necessitated the existence of all that exists. Therefore, sadness, bitterness, lack of desire and choice were the cause of creation. That is why Hindus do not see the world as being real.

5. *What is the relationship between the Hindu god and its creatures? What is the idea of 'self-god'?*

In Hinduism, all that exists is the result of god's manifestation and multiplication. The soul in each individual is identical with god. All creatures are one with god, and they are god. Everybody can say that, "I am god". Anyone who does not believe in the idea of 'self-god' and says, "Brahman is one, and I am another", does not understand.

6. *Why do Hindus believe in many gods? How does the Bible approach the idea of 'self-god'?*

The reason that Hindus believe in many gods (millions) is because everything is the revelation of god. Everybody is god (self-god). This belief has opened the way for people to worship god in whatever form they like. However, the Bible condemns the idea of 'self-god'; *"In the pride of your heart you say, "I am a god; I sit on the throne of a god in the heart of the seas." But you are a man and not a god, though you think you are as wise as a god."* (Ezek. 28:2); *"The Lord is One."* (Deut. 6:4; Mark 12:29).

7. *Can the word 'Reality' be used as synonymous to the Hindu god or 'Brahman'?*

Reality can be attributed only to a God that has personality and is describable, but not to an impersonal god.

8. *Can an impersonal god lead and guide people?*

An impersonal god cannot lead and guide people, since it has no personality to be able to relate to personal beings and thereby describe the purpose, goal and destination or standard of life.

9. *Can an impersonal god manifest itself?*

An impersonal god has no personalities to manifest. The Hindu belief is a contradictory belief. On one hand, it believes that god (Brahman) is an impersonal abstraction that is beyond explanation and cannot be personally defined or described, but on the other hand, it is described as everything that exists.

10. *Hinduism believes in inferior gods and also says that they desire to return to the absolute* *supreme god. Can this transfer happen? Is the idea of inferior gods real?*

This Hindu notion is not real and is completely wrong. A complete God cannot manifest Himself as incomplete inferior beings. However, even if we accept this notion, its own philosophy will prove that it is not real. Inferior compared to the absolute means it is less pure and therefore it is the mixture of good and evil, which proves that inferiors have a personality. In a logical sense, promotion from a dualistic personality to the absolute impersonality is impossible. You cannot say all that exists and has a changing nature and personality can turn into something that will never have personality or become nothing. For example, we cannot say, "*5 persons + 8 persons = 0 person*". In the same way, the 0 person (impersonal being) also is not able to multiply itself into many. The supreme God cannot reveal Himself as a capricious inferior(s). If so, He cannot be called supreme anymore. That is why the Bible believes that God revealed Himself in Jesus Christ with all His fullness (Col. 1:19). As a result, the idea of inferior gods is not supportable.

11. *Is it good for men and women to follow the Hindu god(s)?*

The existence of an evil spirit (or evil god) in the nature of the Hindu god is a problem. It is not advisable for men and women to follow a god that has evil in itself. The Hindu god has two opposite natures (good and evil) and all inferiors that exist came into existence as the result of a collision between these two opposite natures. The darkness or the evil spirit in each person has also come from god. Why would someone follow a god who has given him evil? Can a god that is the cause of evil ask people to do good? On the other hand, just as man is inferior to god, so is the power of the evil spirit in each person inferior when compared to the evil spirit in the supreme god. Why then would a person wish to be absorbed into the absolute god if it means possessing greater evil? Why would someone desire to transfer from a less painful situation to a super painful situation or from less (inferior) darkness to a greater (super) darkness?

12. *Can the Hindu god with the dualistic nature represent the real justice for which the heart of man longs? Can the Hindu god be the source of justice for the world?*

A god with dual nature that is not able to get rid of the desires of its own negative nature and establish the justice within itself cannot be a good example for justice.

13. *Is the Hindu creator, Brahma, eternal?*

No. Brahma is dependent of time. He will die after he completes his age. The universe also endures as long as he lives. The belief in certain age for a creator in Hinduism contradicts its own philosophy that encourages people to be absorbed into eternity. If the creator is not eternal, the works of his hand, including humankind, also will not be able to see eternity.

14. *Why is the position Jesus as Creator and Savior holds superior to Brahma?*

The position Jesus as Creator and Savior holds is superior and incomparable to what Brahma holds. Jesus said, "*Father, glorify me in your presence with the glory I had with you before the world began*" (John 17:5). The Bible states, "*Jesus Christ is the same yesterday and today and forever*" (Heb. 13:8; c.f. Dan. 7:27); He has supreme authority over all things in heaven and on earth (Eph. 1:20-22). This means that He and His heavenly Father exist from eternity before the foundation of the world to eternity. Jesus will live forever and will have His followers with Him forever.

15. *How can the idea of rebirth be against justice?*

The issue of rebirth goes against justice. The idea of rebirth asserts that every crime in the present life is the result of the bad deeds of the previous people who lived before the incarnation. A criminal and a victim were both bad in their previous lives causing them both to be involved in the present crime.

If this is the case, then the social law should not condemn criminals or reward the victims. Because the idea of rebirth is not able to make a distinction between criminals and victims; victims are also criminals at the same time.

However, we know that human conscience and the social laws have clearly distinguished the difference between criminals and victims. When Hindus rise and press hard to gain their human rights, it means that they ignore their religious belief concerning the downfall of their so-called previous self. When someone complains against invaders, it means that he/she does not accept that his/her bad acts in the previous life were the causes of the present invasion. This criticism is applied to the Buddhists too since they also believe in reincarnation.

16. *How is the idea of rebirth a breach to human freedom?*

In Hinduism and Buddhism no one is free from the actions of his/her previous being before the reincarnation. What happens now, what you are now or what you have now has its cause in the previous being. Your previous being before your reincarnation is now the master of your life. You cannot get away from it. You are not free to decide for your own life. Future generations will also not be free from their previous generations. In the same way when we go back to the beginning of creation (or god's multiplication), we see that the evil deeds inside god caused the creation of choiceless people. So the lack of freedom comes from god and is passed from generation to generation forever.

With all these, it is strange that Hinduism teaches the meditation on god in order to reach freedom and perfection. What is freedom or perfection in Hinduism, knowing that even god is neither free nor perfect?

17. *Why does god tie itself to the world by multiplying itself in the form of men and women? Does an authoritative god need self-torture, self-discipline, self-sacrifice, meditation or prayer in order to release itself from the world and achieve perfection and holiness?*

In Hinduism, man's soul (atman) is identical with Brahman (ultimate reality). However, this so-called all-powerful Brahman existing as a man's soul has chained itself to the world and now needs to work hard in order to release itself from the bondage of the world. It has to choose its own path to free its soul from the earthly ties, by way of self-torture, self-discipline, self-sacrifice, hard work, meditation or prayer in order to achieve perfection and holiness. It casts aside everything it might have and closes its eyes to every pleasure of the world, hoping to atone for its sins and reach divinity. Its self is able to create a newer and better man or a divine being for the life after incarnation.

We can see the extent of the contradictory nature of Hindu philosophy; the dualistic nature of god caused division and multiplication inside its own being; therefore god had no choice but to surrender itself to the bondage of inferior multiplications as men and women, to create catastrophic events for itself which can be seen in the daily lives of humanity and now, tries to release itself from the pains which were the result of its own inner unsettlement.

18. *Can Hinduism be a universal model for changing people from self-centeredness into a community of peace?*

In Hinduism man is the center of his own life. Hinduism tries to change man from sociability to self-centeredness by teaching him to deprive himself from any fellowship with others and from all opportunities of social life in order to reach the perfection within him. Therefore, the Hindu model is to separate individuals from the community and make them unsociable.

This is quite opposite to Christianity that rescues people from self-centeredness and brings them into a peaceful relationship with God and with others on earth and in heaven (Col. 1:20). Self-centeredness prevents self giving dedication in a family, society or in the world as a whole. It considers each individual above the community of individuals and therefore causes uncertainty in people's relationships.

19. *Can man be identical with the single spirit of Brahman?*

We have seen that Brahman is not a single spirit but a combination of opposite spirits. However, Hindus say that each person is god, identical with Brahman and will be absorbed into Brahman's oneness.

The existing differences amongst many individuals and amongst many Hindu religious groups prove that there is a difference amongst the individual souls and their productions, and therefore they cannot be identical with a single impersonal spirit (Brahman). The effect of a religious guru or a teacher on others, on the other hand, also has proved that a person in every situation is affected by others and cannot be identical with the so-called unchanging impersonal Brahman. There is a third reason why man cannot be identical with Brahman. Consider the changes that have occurred in Hinduism itself over time, the result of much interference throughout its history. This effect of people and time on each individual is opposite to the Hindu philosophy that believes man is the author of his own life and that he is a self-god with sufficient capacity or capability to protect his identity against change.

20. *Is there a fixed creed in Hinduism that can distinguish the true enlightenment from the false? Who is the final authority to recognize the genuine enlightenment?*

There is not any fixed creed or standard in Hinduism to distinguish the true enlightenment from the false. Transcendence is generated through one's own personal thought and feeling. It is indescribable and indisputable by others or by general wisdom, though everybody is believed to carry the same ultimate reality (Brahman) within him/herself as the source of absolute capacity and capability for understanding and distinguishing.

In Hinduism man is called god, but his eyes, ears, mind, heart and conscience are not able to discover the most genuine belief by comparison. Each person is encouraged to discover the truth from within, in one's own isolated manner, defining and describing it in one's own way. Even though the same so-called absolute god has manifested itself within every one and is the god of all, it does not have a unique enlightenment or heaven for all. Instead, everybody has his/her own enlightenment and heaven. Therefore, each enlightenment is true in itself for that particular self.

The lack of a unique enlightenment in Hinduism contradicts its own belief when it says that all creatures tend to turn to the oneness of god; oneness necessitates a unique enlightenment whereas in Hinduism there are many. Because of this belief, Hinduism is not able to reject atheism and/or to distinguish a difference between theism and polytheism. Because, if every man is the author of his own life in order to create his own creed and enlightenment, his discovery concerning atheism, polytheism or theism must all be called enlightenments.

However, human knowledge and experience have proved that;

- There is a difference between polytheism, theism and atheism; between a religion that believes in reincarnation and impermanence of the soul and one that believes in the independence and permanence of a soul; between someone who is awake and another who is ignorant. Indeed, it is the absence of a unique enlightenment among Hindus that has caused them to believe in many gods.

- The truth cannot be limited to an individual's self or dogma; truth is abundant, unlimited and beyond the boundaries of an individual's thoughts and feelings. Every body needs to discover it in a wider realm.

- The Christian message is powerful when it describes the incapability of man when compared to God; No one is good except God alone (Mark 10:18; Luke 18:19). Therefore, God has already made a distinction between true and false.

21. *Who is the final authority for establishing a way to the ultimate reality in Hinduism and Christianity?*

Hinduism begins and ends with man. Each person is the master of his own life (indeed the master of his future being after reincarnation as we saw in question 16). He is the only authority to establish a way to God.

While man is imperfect, he is asked to create a perfect way to perfection!! This is impossible. The Bible says;

> *They* (people) *are zealous for God, but their zeal is not based on knowledge. Since they did not know the righteousness that comes from God and sought to establish their own, they did not submit to God's righteousness* (Rom.10:2-3).
>
> *You do not have, because you do not ask God* (Jms.4:2c).

Christianity begins and ends with God. God is the perfect and unchangeable standard for imperfect, unrighteous and changeable man. Perfect God creates a perfect path that leads to righteousness and perfection, but imperfect man cannot lead his life to perfection. God is the source and builder of the perfect life. Only He can save.

Man Is the Creator of God in Buddhism

Background

Buddhism was founded in India about 500 B.C. by Buddha. Buddha was born in southern Nepal. His real name was Siddhartha Gautama. He was a devoted Hindu and sought enlightenment (bodhi) through extreme self-denial and self-torture. He was not successful with such practices and therefore abandoned them and started the search through a *Middle Way*, which is based on the mind and meditation in order to resist the evil life and gain happiness and peace. He said that he experienced enlightenment through his new discovery; his followers therefore called him Buddha, which means 'awakened or enlightened one'.

Buddha did not teach his disciples to be dependent upon a supreme being, but his later followers deified and worshipped him. There is no evidence in his preachings to show that he rejected the existence of gods, however he did not consider them important. He taught that people are simply links in the Wheel of Life; they are born, live and die according to the laws of nature. This is like a seed that lies in the ground, becomes a plant, wilts and disappears and like water that turns into steam, rises up to become clouds and then brings forth water. He based his belief on the significance of man and believed that each person was able to save him/herself through his Noble Eight Fold Path. For this reason he spent his whole life ministering to his disciples so they could learn the way of success.

Buddha believed that nothing was permanent; all things were transitory and subject to change. In the Buddhist doctrine of *anatta* (which means 'no-soul'), unlike other religions, there is no soul for a man; there is nothing more to man than what we see and know of him. Man is made of the body (*rupa*), feeling or sensation (*vedana*), ideas (*sanna*), mental processes and acts (*sankhara*) and awareness or consciousness (*vinnana*); neither one of these nor the sum of them has any soul. Because there is no reality behind such a word, life is soulless or selfless; no one can have a fixed identity because of continual change. This will be discussed in further detail in the "question and answer" section.

Dharma

Dharma is Buddha's teaching, which means 'saving truth'. Buddha teaches that existence is an endless cycle of death and rebirth; man is born, dies and is born again. Therefore, every individual has more than one existence. Buddha believes that existence is the cause of suffering. This means that men and women may not be able to release themselves from this painful world. The only possible escape is nirvana[7] (enlightenment) that takes you to eternal release from the cycle of death and birth. This discussion will be centered on whether or not

---

[7] *Nirvana* means going out of misery and entering into perfect peace and happiness.

nirvana is possible by human power, the power that arises from the so-called selfless body of Buddhism.

Each person's position and well-being in life is determined by his/her behavior in the previous life; good deeds may lead to rebirth as a wise and wealthy person or as a being in heaven, and evil deeds may lead to rebirth as a poor and sickly person or even to rebirth in hell. To escape from a painful and continuous cycle of death and rebirth and to achieve enlightenment, people have to free themselves of all fleshly desires and cravings and of all worldly dependence.

Buddha based his teachings on four things believed to open the way to a new life; recognizing the existence of pain, the cause of pain[8], the need to avoid the cause of pain, and the way of ending the pain - which is Buddha's Eight Fold Path. The Eight Fold Path contains his ethical teachings: right understanding (of pain, its origin and cause, the way to freedom), right resolve (thought free from evil), right speaking, right action, right means of maintaining life, right effort, right mindfulness (being aware of negatives), and right concentration (concentration on the truth only). He believed that this Eight Fold Path leads to purity; he asked his disciples to enter this path and make an end to suffering.

---

[8] Craving is the origin of pain and suffering. Liberation occurs after craving is completely faded away and extinguished.

Throughout the teachings of Buddha, there are not gods, and therefore no veneration or worship to any god and accordingly no religious ceremonies. In his teaching, he never claims any inspiration from any god or divine power. His ministry was only to teach his disciples to rely on their own intelligence in order to get rid of pain and attain enlightenment. It seems that he did not find gods relevant to his teaching since man was asked to be the master of his own life. This does not mean that he did not believe that supernatural beings existed. He may have believed in gods but may have not accepted them as good examples for humankind, particularly when they indulged in sensual pleasures and quarreled with one another. He may have thought of them as unqualified in helping man to reach nirvana. This is because he believed in the impermanence and nothingness of all that exists, including all divine beings. However, despite Buddha's silence about gods, some of his followers (Mahayanists) revised his teachings with the absolutist notion of ultimate reality and presented it as a rational religion.

Sects

Certain Buddhist sects began to develop in Asian countries after the death of its founder, Buddha. They do have similarities and do share many common values, but they also vary in some important areas because of the influences made by outsiders throughout history. The close study of two major sects of Buddhism *Theravada*, the conservative form and *Mahayana*[9], the liberal form will enable us to have a more thorough understanding of all other Buddhist sects:

1. *Theravada* means *Way or Doctrine of the Elders* (Mahayanist call it *Lesser Vehicle or Course*). *Theravada* claims that it alone holds to the original message of Buddha and has no interest in any alteration. It teaches man to reach his goal (nirvana) on his own and there is no one, neither any god nor any man, to help him. He alone is the lamp and refuge for his own salvation. He must hold firm to the instruction of Buddha in order to conquer the causes of pain and reach the state of liberation. It also teaches that Buddha is not divine as many Mahayanists believe he is, but just a man with great wisdom who reached nirvana and then passed on the knowledge of his experience to his followers. There is neither a god, nor a spiritual or material substance that exists by itself as the ultimate reality. The world as we know it does not have its origin in a primordial being such as Brahman in Hinduism, it exists only in the minds of those who perceive it. All that exists is unreal and insubstantial; the product of the mind. When the mind stops thinking, and awareness disappears, all that exists is said to have ceased to be. The ultimate reality is the truth that surpasses and governs all that exists.

---

[9] *Theravada* is dominant in south-east Asian countries of Sri Lanka, Burma/ Myanmar, Thailand and Laos. Mahayana is dominant in the northern countries of Nepal, Tibet, Vietnam, China, Korea and Japan.

2. *Mahayana* means *Great Vehicle to Salvation.* Mahayana Buddhists base their belief on the interpretation of Buddha's disciples. They believe that the disciples were capable of sensing Buddha's revelation in its real meaning because they were his chosen ones. They lived with him, saw him and heard him face to face; they were Buddha's direct and real messengers who experienced life with him.

A vast majority of Buddhists belong to the Mahayana sect. Mahayanists are more liberal compared to the Theravadins and have a revised version of the original doctrines of Buddha. They teach that man is not alone and that everybody can gain salvation by good works, and also by seeking help and guidance from human and supernatural beings. They see Buddha as having three different forms; as the man Gautama who achieved enlightenment, as a human being who became divine, and as the absolute and eternal reality that transcends all limiting conditions. As a divine being Buddha works through other savior Buddhas or Gurus in the lives of people to promote their spirituality.

Compared to Theravada, Mahayana takes a Hindu Pantheistic approach, describing ultimate reality with two distinct aspects - relative and absolute. The relative aspect is the representative of the absolute and adapts to earthly conditions in order to relieve people from suffering and lead them to liberation.

Since Mahayana Buddhism is closely related to Hinduism, the questions and answers below are based on Theravada Buddhism to avoid duplication.

Questions & Answers

1. *What characteristics of the gods may have caused Buddha to ignore or to consider them less important?*

In Hinduism, Buddha saw that gods were self-destructive, involved in fighting and sensual pleasures, had a transitory nature, were incomplete, impermanent, having a negative effect on people. This may have caused Buddha to see them as unreliable and bad examples for humankind.

2. *Can man be his own light and refuge? Can man put away all his cravings, extinguish them all within himself and reach perfect liberation?*

In Buddhism, like Hinduism, but unlike Christianity, man is the master of his own life. He is the source and authority of his own faith. Therefore, if every person is the master of his own life, a craving, therefore, might not be called a craving in another person's mind. Therefore, Buddha's instructions cannot play the role of a fixed creed in other people's lives.

Secondly, in Buddhism faith is made in the mind of man who is transitory. Therefore, the truth about that faith is discovered in the mind of man not in the revelation of an absolute reality or a unique God as Christianity believes. Since Buddha has called everything relative, transitory and unreal, man's effort for salvation also is relative and unreal. He therefore cannot be his own real light and refuge. He needs a real light outside his life in order to open his life to the real life or enlightenment.

Also, for Buddha enlightenment is the state of perfect liberation. If someone, who is called the master of his own life, has not reached the state of perfect liberation, it means that he is imperfect. We know that imperfection never leads to perfection. It is only the perfect that can lead to perfection.

Lastly, it is also impossible for a man to extinguish all cravings in his mind and heart. Since he alone is the master of his own life he is also the creator or the cause and gratifier of his cravings. How can he be trusted as a savior while he is the source and gratifier of his own pain? Secondly, the history of human experience has proven that the powers of temptation that have imprisoned mankind are above and beyond human power. If, on the other hand, man had greater power than temptation, they would have the ability to overcome, not succumb, to it, leaving great lessons of confidence and hope for future generations. However, this is not the case since history has only ever heard of one who has successfully defeated human cravings, Jesus Christ (read Eph.2:1-10).

3. *Is the view of peace and happiness presented in Buddhism absolute or relative? How might one know when he has achieved peace and happiness (Nirvana)?*

In Buddhism everything exists when it is conceived in the mind. When the mind stops and awareness fades away everything disappears. Therefore, peace and happiness, like everything that exists, are not absolute but relative. Even though Buddha talked about enlightenment, his "relative philosophy" cannot present an absolute enlightenment. If something is relative it means it might not be right. Therefore, no one can be certain of achieving peace and happiness.

4. *Is the Eight Fold Path sufficient enough to lead someone to attain perfect peace and happiness? What obstacles stand in the way of achieving happiness and peace?*

We know that each person in the world is able to discipline him/herself to be good to some extent by following a set of instructions, but no one is completely able to extinguish all evil desires from his/her heart. This will be much more evident in the case of Buddhism which offers no divine aid, where there is no power beyond your own thought to empower you. On the other hand, Buddha rejected the permanence and eternal entity of 'self', believing it only to be a figment of our imagination. Therefore, reaching perfect peace and happiness means to reach the nothingness of all and self. In other words, a person who continually becomes emptied of Buddhist imaginary 'self' cannot use the self identifying pronoun 'I' and therefore is not able to say that 'I' can be attentive to the Eight Fold Path and consequently cannot concentrate on the real truth. Thirdly, if everything is unreal in the world, Buddha's discovery of pain and his Eight Fold Path also must be unreal. Because it is the product of Buddha's meditation in relation to the pain caused by the unreal and insubstantial world, the pain of the unreal world is unreal, therefore, the resolution for that pain also is unreal.

5. *Does Buddhism believe in the existence of any real thing in the world?*

For Buddhism everything is unreal and insubstantial. It exists only because you think it exists.

6. *Is Buddhism able to introduce a universal faith of peace and happiness?*

Buddhism was founded on the limited mind of man whom it believes has become the cause of all pains and sufferings. If man is the cause of every pain, his faith and every product of his mind also carry the pain and suffering within themselves. Therefore, man who is the cause of every pain is not able to create and introduce a universal faith that can give peace and happiness to people. Secondly, Buddhism has omitted the 'soul' of mankind from its philosophy and therefore its instructions of faith (Eight Fold Path) do not cover all the dimensions of life. Therefore, it cannot be complete in its approach to human need of peace and happiness. Thirdly, Buddhism believes in the nothingness (emptiness) of all that exists. Accordingly, any idea, including Buddha's teaching, which comes from nothingness in man must be nothing. Fourthly, Buddhism believes that everything is the product of the mind; when the mind stops working everything disappears. Therefore faith can have no permanent value.

7. *What is the difference between Christianity and Buddhism?*

The greatest difference is in the area of hope. In Buddhism, when you become empty of everything and lose your hope in all that exists, including every divine power, you attain the peace and happiness that are only defined into the limited and relative boundary of an individual. The perception of peace and happiness in one individual's eyes will not be the same as another individual's. Man needs an absolute standard of peace and happiness in order to effectively achieve genuine peace and happiness amongst all individuals. In Christianity you are transferred from unstable human hope to eternal hope, from individual and self-centered happiness and peace to eternal happiness and peace which are the result of reconciliation and togetherness of all that exist in heaven and on earth (2Cor. 5:18-21; Col. 1:20).

A second difference is the soul of mankind. Buddhism believes man is soulless or selfless, but Christianity believes that man has an eternal soul, so that the permanent nature of the soul may link him to eternal peace and happiness (Matt. 25:46; John 5:24; Rom. 2:7; 6:23).

Buddha's philosophy of 'no soul' is illogical and goes against itself. If life is the continuous cycle of death and rebirth, and if man is nothing more than what we see, then what part of man will carry itself to the next reincarnation or rebirth? If soul or self is imaginary, likewise consciousness, pain, suffering, and salvation are also imaginary; even Buddha's teachings become imaginary and unreal. Secondly, if no one has a fixed identity, Buddha's Eight Fold Path cannot be applied as a fixed instruction to other people and later generations since he himself did not have a fixed identity. If life is soulless or selfless, then good or bad, salvation or lack of salvation does not make sense. Also, Buddha said that everything including the immaterial things such as essence and feeling is created by the human mind. If these things are the products of the mind, why then is it that the soul cannot be the product of the mind and remain in Buddha's imaginary file? If the word "soul" is not the product of the mind, then how is it that this word exists in Buddha's vocabulary? Could it be that his mind had created the notion of a soul yet he refused to accept it?

A third difference is that in Christianity, God is not the product of man's mind. Instead, He is Mighty and the Creator of all. As a Christian, you cannot look around nature, see beautiful creatures around you and simply say, 'they are not real, are nothing, do not exist and only the mind thinks that they exist'. Their existence challenges your mind to use logic, to search and to find the real Creator of all. How is that Buddha saw all things around him but called them 'nothing and unreal'; he couldn't 'see' his own 'mind', but called the work of his mind as set out in his Eight Fold Path real and practicable for all!

8. *Can anyone with a dualistic nature (the mixture of good and bad) explore his inner being and find a way into pure enlightenment?*

Dualism is the arena of bondage, sadness and hostility, but enlightenment, as we expect, is the arena of absolute liberation, peace and happiness. Therefore, there cannot be any relationship between dualism and enlightenment. No one can reach freedom, happiness and peace while he is in the bondage of sadness and hostility. Release from spiritual bondage into freedom is not a gradual process either; freedom is a complete release that occurs in a moment. A moment ago you were in bondage but now you are free. You cannot say that you are free but still be under some bondage. Freedom is complete; it does not come bit by bit. As a result, the liberation in all world religions, except Christianity, is not real since they rely on man's gradual effort to release himself. However, in Christianity when you ask the prince of light, Jesus Christ, to release you from the hands of the prince of darkness, Satan, He immediately listens to your call and releases you from the bondage of Satan. In order to think, speak and act properly, you firstly need to be released from the bondage of evil, a powerful force in dualistic life. As a result, a dualistic life does not lead to pure enlightenment.

9. *Buddhism always regards suffering as something bad. How does Christianity see suffering?*

Christian Scriptures tell us that God brings good out of suffering in the lives of believers (Rom. 8:17-18; 2Cor. 1:5-6; 1Pet. 4:12-14; 5:10). The suffering of Christ provided salvation for the world (Heb. 5:8-9; 9:26; 13:12; 1Pet. 3:18).

Paul, the disciple of Christ says;

> *See what this godly sorrow has produced in you: what earnestness, what eagerness to clear yourselves,...what readiness to see*

> *justice done. At every point you have proved yourselves to be innocent in this matter* (2Cor.7:11).

With many trials and pains in his life journeys, Paul learned that in order to prove his love toward Christ he needed to go through many trials and hardships (2Cor.11:23-28). His words bring forth the meaning that sometimes it is not the lack of suffering but rather the presence of suffering in our lives that gives satisfaction (Rom.8:35-39; 1Thes.1:6-7).

Also, parents are motivated by love to suffer for the sake of their children so that their children might be able to avoid or escape from some risk or danger.

Darkness and Light Are Complementary in Taoism

Background

Taoism[10] is a polytheistic religion that arose in China sometime between 500 B.C. and 300 B.C. Even though Taoism probably arose earlier than the major sects of Buddhism, it has borrowed many of its ideas from Mahayana Buddhism. There are two types of Taoism; religious and philosophical. Religious Taoism has ceremonies that are mixtures of animism[11], polytheism and occultism, but philosophical Taoism does not have a formalized worship of deities. It only encourages people to be in harmony with the laws of nature.

Yin and Yang

On one hand, Taoism believes in the immutability and unchanging nature of supreme reality, Tao, who existed before heaven and the earth, on the other hand it believes in Tao as the source of multiplicity and all forms of manifestations.

Taoism believes that '*Yin* and *Yang*' are two opposite and at the same time complementary characters that flow down from Tao (god) into every

---

[10] *Tao* (pronounced 'Dao') means 'way', 'the way the universe works', or 'the absolutely real'. The word *Tao* was used in Chinese Bible as an equivalent word for *Logos* (or Word) in John 1:1. Taoism is practised in Singapore, Indonesia, Thailand, Hong Kong, Taiwan and Hawaii.

[11] Animism believes that all the physical world including trees, stones, stars, and other objects carry the spiritual forces that have penetrated them. Animism has made its way into many religious beliefs around the world and is strongly evident in folk religions.

inferior spiritual and material being. Yin is the female principle of darkness, passivity and regression; Yang is the male principle of light, activity and progress.

Though darkness (Yin) and light (Yang) are enemies, Taoists believe that neither one should be destroyed. To them all aspects of life in the world are in harmony; masculine with feminine, hard with soft, hot with cold, light with dark, good with evil, right with wrong, true with false, big with small, black with white, etc. Even though they are different in nature, they correlate with each other. They exist together in perfect harmony, because the supreme power is in control of Yin and Yang and brings all these aspects in harmony with each other. For this reason, a Taoist must do everything calmly and welcome the consequences whatever they be good or bad because his self or inner being is in perfect harmony with Tao. To avoid trouble, Taoists should not chase the pleasures of the world and upset the balance between Yin and Yang. Instead, they should live quietly and peacefully under the laws of nature and should not make any moral judgments or act against any aspect of nature and therefore create disharmony in their life.

Questions & Answers

1. *What is the major problem with Taoism? How would you compare it with Christianity?*

Taoism, unlike Christianity, believes that supreme reality is impersonal. An impersonal god cannot have any mind, heart, character or attributes that are needed in order to have a relationship with people. You cannot say that an impersonal god creates, calls, instructs, leads, encourages, is knowable and accessible. You cannot attribute any relational characteristic to him (or it) because he is impossible to relate to. How can you then follow an impersonal god?

Secondly, Tao is the creator of both good and evil. Instead of rescuing people from evil, he himself has created evil and furthermore has called people to bow down to it. For this reason, salvation has no meaning in Taoism. In Christianity, God is not the creator of evil. He rejects evil and rescues people from it.

Thirdly, Taoism encourages passivity towards evil and rejects human activity in every dimension of life against evil. "Evil" is thought of as complementary to "good", not opposite. Christianity, unlike Taoism, sees "evil" as enemy to "good", therefore encourages assertiveness, which promotes people to reject the evil spirit (John 8:32; Rom. 12:9; 1Thes. 5: 21; Heb. 5:14; 1John 4:1-3).

2. *In what way will Taoism block the establishment of equal opportunity and the advancement of women in society?*

Taoism attributes the darkness, passivity and regression aspects of life to *Yin* and calls it the **female** gender of the law of nature, whereas all positive aspects of live are attributed to *Yang* and is called the **male** gender of the law of nature. This has affected the place of women negatively in society. People call them shy, unassertive, narrow-minded, disorganized and hard to work with and use these words as a subtle excuse to block their promotion in society. Though laws support the equal treatment of males and females, the enforcement of those laws will be hard because of the negative view of people's belief towards women.

Satan Is as Mighty as God in Zoroastrianism

Background

Zoroastrianism is not a widespread religion in the contemporary world. It was the religion of the country of Iran before Islam. After Muslims invaded Iran, the numbers of Zoroastrians started to decline. Many of them did not want to convert into Islam and therefore escaped to India and took asylum there. A large number of Zoroastrians live in India now.

Zoroastrianism was included in this book for discussion because some believe that Christianity, like Judaism, Islam and Mahayana Buddhism, has borrowed some values from it. This comparison aims to prove that Christianity is based on a Holy God, whereas Zoroastrianism worships a dualistic god.

Zoroaster was the ancient Iranian (Persian) prophet who lived in Iran during the sixth century B.C. a little earlier than Buddha in India. He called people to follow the true wise god, 'Ahura Mazda (or Ohrmazd)', against the evil god 'Ahriman (Angra Mainyu or Satan)' by the way of right thoughts, right speech and right deeds. However, Zoroastrian texts show that there are other gods that aim to help people in various conditions.

Two Gods Opposing One Another

Zoroaster believed that Ahura Mazda and Ahriman were two gods opposing one another and both were eternal and all-powerful. Ahura Mazda created the world so that with its assistance, he could achieve his aim to overthrow Ahriman.

Zoroastrians believe that the equality of power in both God and Satan is a sign of people's absolute freedom of will in choosing either. If one is all-powerful, then people tend to lean towards the one who has the greater power. This will eliminate their free will.

However, it is the equality of power in God and Satan that leaves no place for people to practice their free will. The logic behind this assumption is that if the so-called all-powerful Satan rises up to take control over people, then God will not be able to unchain them since His power is no greater than that of Satan.

Zoroaster claimed that the truth was revealed to him by Ahura Mazda. Ahura Mazda revealed this to him in order to send him as his prophet amongst the people to teach them to reject idolatry and to pay homage only to him.

Zoroastrianism also believes in various good and bad spirits. Some of the ancient Iranian deities are also regarded as worthy of worship, though subordinate to Ahura Mazda. They are regarded as helpers and protectors in times of hardship. For this reason, Zoroastrianism is called a mixture of monotheism, polytheism and dualism.

Zoroastrianism also believes in the coming of a savior in the final days, the Day of Resurrection for final judgment and a life after death in heaven or hell. In the life after death, the righteous – the one whose right deeds outweigh his bad deeds - will be able to pass over a tiny bridge as thin as a single hair and enter heaven, but the unrighteous will remain in hell.

The problem arises here, as it is in Islam, that the Zoroastrian god takes his righteous followers straight to hell, Satan's territory, after death and makes them go through the ordeal of proving to him that they can cross over to heaven on a narrow bridge. What is this test meant to prove? Is this meant to show god who is righteous and who is not? Does he not already know the righteous from the unrighteous? Also, if god really does love the righteous why does he make them pass through hell and taste its bitterness? Why does Satan allow those righteous in hell to cross over to heaven? Is the so-called all-powerful Satan willing to release those within his territory?

<u>Questions & Answers</u>

1. *What is the problem in Zoroastrianism?*

Zoroastrianism believes in two absolute ultimate beings, Ahura Mazda (God) and Ahriman (Satan), which is impossible.

2. *Will we be able to call God omnipotent, omnipresent and omniscient if Satan is attributed with the same qualities?*

No! They are the qualities of only one infinite Ultimate Reality. Logically, we cannot say that, 'there are two infinite ultimate realities'. The word "ultimate" refers to an extremity, a perfection, beyond which there is nothing at all. In mathematical language also we cannot say that 'there are two infinites' because two infinites is like one infinity ($\infty + \infty = \infty$). As a result, there is only one Ultimate Reality that has the above qualities with absolute truth and justice. If God is not superior to Satan, as in Zoroastrianism, there will never be any hope for salvation, happiness and peace.

3. *Is there an end to Ahriman (Satan)?*

Nothing can happen to him if he is called all-powerful (omnipotent). This means, there is no end for his evil threats; there will not be a single time of peace and comfort for Ahura Mazda and his followers even in paradise. If Ahriman is as powerful as Ahura Mazda, nothing can stop him from entering paradise. Therefore, the Zoroastrian paradise will never be immune to the eternal presence and might of the evil spirit, Ahriman. In fact, in Zoroastrian paradise (similar to Islamic paradise) we can see the sign of Ahriman (Satan). In these religions, men and women's entry to paradise is based on their good deeds outweighing their bad deeds, but not on a pure righteousness, each person thereby carries some darkness, though little but still the sign of Satan, into paradise. This will be discussed in detail in the concluding section.

4. *What is the difference between Zoroastrianism and Christianity?*

In Zoroastrianism God is equal to Satan and cannot overcome him. Therefore, any hope for salvation is unachievable. In Christianity God is mightier than Satan, has overcome him and prepared the way of salvation for everyone who believes in Him. Jesus said;

> *My Father is greater than all, no one can snatch them* (Christians) *out of my Father's hand. I and the Father are one* (Jn.10:29-30).

> *Take heart! I have overcome the world* (Jn.16:23).

Another difference is that in Zoroastrianism the righteous must pass through the gates of hell on their way to heaven after death. However, in Christianity God is always, before and after death, keeping His righteous away from the claws of Satan, *and the gates of Hades will not overcome them* (Mt.16:18).

God Inspired Sin in Islam

Background

Islam was founded in 610 A.D. by Muhammad in Mecca, Saudi Arabia. Muhammad claimed to be the prophet of Allah who revealed the Qur'an[12] (Koran) to him. Muhammad rose up against polytheism and claimed that Allah was the one true God.

Allah was the name of the superior idol worshipped in Saudi Arabia; it was a name familiar to many nations. Muhammad adopted the name 'Allah' for his own monotheistic purpose in order to arrest people's attention. He claimed himself to be the last and greatest prophet of all, and the Qur'an as the holiest book on earth. He proclaimed Satan as a deceiver, believed in heaven and hell, in the Day of Judgment, and preached that the unrighteous would go to hell and the righteous to heaven. Nevertheless, the righteous on their way to heaven must first go to hell and then try entering heaven.

Islam is the second largest religion in the world. Two major divisions in Islam are Sunni and Shi'a. There are also many subdivisions amongst both Sunnis and Shiites. Approximately, 80% of Muslims belong to Sunnis sects.

The major reason for the division between the two sects was due to a disagreement concerning succession among the leaders after the death of

---

[12] Muhammad's associates preserved his teachings by memorizing or writing them down during his lifetime. Later, the materials of his teaching were collected and made into a book, called "the Qur'an".

Muhammad. After Muhammad's death, Ali, the son-in-law and cousin of Muhammad, believed his family line to be the rightful successors. However, Muhammad's three father-in-laws united against Ali's expectation, declaring that the eldest among them must succeed Muhammad. This was a major point of contention between the two groups, leading to the ultimate division of the Shiite and Sunni.

Shiites call Ali and his descendants 'Imam' (leader) and sinless. The major Shiite sect, which is called 'Twelvers', believe that there were twelve Imams, beginning with 'Ali' and ending with Al-Mahdi. They believe that Al-Mahdi did not die, but hid himself and will reappear on the last day to restore justice and righteousness to the world. Concerning the final day, Sunnis follow more of a Qur'anic teaching that Jesus will come again and judge the world in the end (Q. 3:55; 4: 158).

Similar to Zoroastrianism, Islam also believes that after death both righteous and unrighteous will enter hell. It is from hell that those whose good deeds outweigh their bad will pass over a narrow bridge, as thin as a single hair, and enter heaven. The unrighteous, though, will remain in hell (Q.19:68, 71-72).

This is not just and reasonable - that the righteous on his way to paradise is to be first placed in hell by Allah. Why is it that Allah punishes the obedient, allowing them to experience the terrible pain of hell? This is a clear indication to the misleading nature of Islamic doctrine.

Also worth noting is the Qur'anic statements with regards to the Christian Trinity. It writes that those who believe in God as triune and Jesus as God, are unbelievers and belong to hell (Q.5: 17, 73; 9: 29-30; 66: 9). Contrary to these verses, the Qur'an also states that the Word and Spirit of God came to Mary and formed a perfect and holy man, Jesus (Q.4:171; 19:17, 19). The phrases "Word of God", "Spirit of God" and "Perfect and Holy Man" highlight the fact that God did reveal Himself as Jesus.

Partnership with Sin

Though Muslims believe in the uniqueness, purity and holiness of Allah, the statements in the Qur'an about the inspiration of sin in man and Satan by Allah prove the opposite (Q.7:16-18,179; 9:51; 57:22; 91:7-9);

> *By a Soul and Him* (Allah) *who balanced it, And breathed into its wickedness* (debauchery in Arabic) *and its piety* (Q.91:7-8).

> *He* (Satan) *said* (to Allah), *'Now, for that you has caused me to err, surely in your straight path will I lay wait for them* (humankind)*: Then I will surely come upon them from before, and from behind, and from their right hand, and from their left, and you shall*

> *not find the greater part of them to be thankful.' He said, 'Go forth from it, a scorned, a banished one! Whoever of them shall follow you, I will surely fill hell with you, one and all'* (Q. 7:16-18).

How strange that verses 7 and 8 of chapter 91 of the Qur'an say that Allah has filled man's soul with sin but verse 9 of the same chapter says that anyone who purifies himself will prosper. These are the major doctrinal problems in the Qur'an. Firstly, man will not be able to purify the mighty sin that has been inspired by Allah. Secondly, the call of Allah is not just, since he has filled man's heart with sin and caused him to commit sin. Chapter 7 also states another similar problem caused by Allah. He has corrupted Satan to capture men and women for hell.

Despite all these hardships that Allah himself has created for men and women, he has called them to act righteous if they want to prosper. The question that can be raised here is, "Are they able to act righteous in any way if Allah has ordained them to be sinners?" The answer is, "They are disabled by Allah and they cannot act righteous". However, even if they were able to do good, Allah has yet again laid another obstacle in their path to eternity. He is not pleased to take them directly to heaven or paradise, rather desiring to first place them in hell;

> *Man saith: 'What! after I am dead, shall I in the end be brought forth alive? Doth not*

> *man bear in mind that we made him at first, when he was nought? And I swear by the Lord, we will surely gather together them and the Satans: then will we set them on their knees round Hell: Then will we take forth from each band those of them who have been stoutest in rebellion against the God of Mercy: Then shall we know right well to who its burning is most due: No one is there of you who shall not go down unto it –this is a settled decree with thy Lord- Then will we deliver those who had the fear of God, and the wicked will we leave in it on their knees* (Q.19:66-72).

> *...His* (Allah's) *angels intercede for you* (Muslims), *that He may bring you forth out of darkness into light* (Q.33:43).

This must be the most shocking religious decree the world has experienced ever since the rise of humankind. Why does Allah call himself the "God of Mercy" despite all the pain he inflicts on man, even the righteous? Why does Allah blame man for their rebellion, if he himself has desired and created man to be rebellious (sinner)? Why would a god, if he is merciful, treat the righteous in the same manner as the unrighteous? Is this the Qur'an definition of "Mercy"? If the mercy of Allah does not protect a righteous Muslim from the bitterness of hell, what else may be deduced but that this mercy is false?

The above verses have been the cause of chaos in Islamic doctrine since the rise of Islam. They prove that Allah's purpose in creation for humanity was not for a peaceful life on earth and a joyful life in eternity.

The Islamic traditions (*Hadiths*[13] in Arabic) narrate that Muhammad claimed Allah's purpose and pleasure in creation was for man to commit sin. Even if Muhammad would not want to commit sin, Allah would sweep him out of existence and replace him by one who commits sin and then seeks forgiveness from Allah.[14] Allah has thrown man

---

[13] Hadiths are the writings about Muhammad's and his companions' sayings and deeds, which guide Muslims in founding their social laws and governments, and also in conducting their daily lives. According to the Qur'an, Muslims see themselves obliged to imitate Muhammad's example (cf. Q.4:80; 7:157; 14:44; 33:21).

[14] **a.** Sahih Al-Musim Hadith No.1277
Narrated Abu Ayyub Anasari: Abu Salimah reported that when the time of death of Abu Ayyub drew near, he said: I used to conceal from you a thing which I heard from Allah's Apostle (peace be upon him) and I heard Allah's Apostle (peace be upon him) as saying: Had you not committed sins, Allah would have brought into existence a creation that would have committed sin (and Allah) would have forgiven them.

b. Sahih Al-Musim Hadith No.1278
Narrated Abu Hurayrah: Allah's Apostle (peace be upon him) said: By Him in whose Hand is my life, if you were not to commit sin, Allah would sweep you out of existence and He would replace (you by) those people who would commit sin and seek forgiveness from Allah, and He would have pardoned them.

into the fire of sin. In response, the righteous cry out, praying for release five times a day, doing whatever Allah has wished, killing whoever Allah has decreed in order to persuade him to rescue them from the penalty of sin, but to no avail.

Allah's ordination of man with sin and his creed for all Muslims to visit hell has left a terrifying and uncertain life for Muslims. They are uncertain of their salvation no matter how well they have performed their religious task and served Allah. If you ask the most righteous Muslim, "Will you go to heaven after death?" He will respond, "I don't know." Uncertainty is an inseparable part of Islamic doctrine. Even Muhammad was uncertain of his future;

> *Neither know I what will be done with me or you. Only what is revealed to me do I follow, and I am only charged to warn you* (Q.46:9).

Logically speaking, we know that the pure and holy God has no partnership with sin and cannot create sin because of His pure nature. The Holy God desires the well-being of His people. He does not lead the righteous to hell. However, the Qa'ran and the Islamic traditions state the opposite and in this way put the oneness and holiness of Allah under question. Any god who creates sin and takes pleasure in people's wrongdoing and suffering cannot be real; rather a dualistic god created in the image of man, taking pleasure in the sin and pain of others.

<u>Allah's Paradise: Before and Now!</u>

The verses in the Qur'an prove that Allah's paradise (heaven) previously had no tolerance for sin but now tolerates many sins. This latter Qur'anic belief contradicts Allah's reason for forcing Adam and Eve out of the Garden of Eden.

We know from the Qur'an that Adam and Eve were expelled from the Garden of Eden by Allah after they first sinned. Allah could no longer bear their dualistic and sinful nature in the Garden of Eden and drove them out of his presence. However, the situation has changed now; people can enter paradise despite the impurity of their souls. How can Allah allow men and women to enter paradise carrying their impurity, when Adam and Eve were banished because of a single sin? The following Qur'anic verses clearly prove the above contradiction:

> *And we* (God) *said, 'O Adam! dwell you and your wife in the Garden, and eat plentifully there from wherever you wish; but to this tree do not approach, lest you become of the transgressors.' But Satan made them slip from it, and caused their banishment from the place in which they were. And we said, 'Get you down, the one of you an enemy to the other: and there shall be for you in the earth a dwelling-place, and provision for a time.'* (Q. 2: 35-36).

> *Surely, therefore, will we call those to account, to whom an Apostle has been sent, and of the sent ones themselves will we certainly demand a reckoning. And with knowledge will we tell them of their deeds, for we were not absent from them. The weighing on that day, with justice! and they whose balances shall be heavy, these are they who shall be happy. And they whose balances shall be light, these are they who have lost their souls, for that to our signs they were unjust* (Q. 7: 6-9).

The verses Q. 2:35-36 clearly prove that Adam and Eve sinned only once and for this one sin they were called impure. They were separated from Allah and forced out of the Garden of Eden. Only one sin harmed their souls and made them immoral and unfit for Allah's paradise. He could not forgive them even though their good deeds far outweighed their bad. So it can be seen that the ancient paradise was totally against sin and would not tolerate it. On the contrary, verses Q. 7: 6-9 bring forth the meaning that Allah has become more receptive in his approach to sin. He is no longer as extreme as he was with Adam and Eve. Even people with impurity are allowed to enter paradise, on the condition that their good deeds are "heavy" and their bad deeds are "light". This lenient Allah is the very same who previously could not tolerate the one sin of Adam and Eve. This proves that Allah's moral law is not always absolute and cannot remain the same for all time and eternity. At the beginning, the moral law ordained by Allah considered even a single sin as the enemy of virtue and demanded man to be absolutely moral. But now it does not demand man to be absolutely moral, instead relatively moral which is the combination of 'good and bad', in which the good outweighs the bad. Truth cannot be absolute at one time and relative in another. We cannot call the Truth relative, because it is the denial of the Truth.

Questions & Answers

1. *What are the major problems in Islam?*

In the Qur'an, Allah is the creator and cause of sin. Sin is inspired by Allah in humankind and Satan. Also, Allah takes the righteous Muslims first to hell, the territory of Satan, and then the righteous will try to release themselves from hell and enter heaven. The condition for a righteous Muslim to enter heaven is that his good deeds should outweigh his bad. This is another major problem in Islam; that sinners can enter and contaminate heaven with sin.

2. *If Allah, as the ultimate reality in Islam, is the cause of sin, how would a Muslim then be able to overcome sin and its terrible penalty, hell?*

It seems that the destiny of Muslims is with sin and its penalty. As long as they remain with Allah and obey him, they will not be able to remove the power of sin and its consequence over their life. On one hand, Allah has made Muslims unrighteous and vulnerable by inspiring sin in them to become unable to avoid sin and stand for/in righteousness. On the other hand, he has ordained Satan with sin in order to take advantage of their vulnerability and weaknesses and trap them for hell (Q.91:7-8; Q. 7:16-18).

3. *How could Allah ask Muslims to not sin if he has ordained them to sin? Is Allah really interested in giving people a chance to act in accordance with the truth?*

This is one of the contradicting calls of the Qur'an and cannot be just. It is as if a parent was to encourage his child and sends him/her to steal things, but after, judges or condemns the child of stealing. If Allah on one hand falls in favor with the sin and drives it into the hearts of Muslims and encourages them to sin, why would he on the other hand ask Muslims not to sin?

4. *Can a genuine God inspire sin?*

No! It is impossible for a genuine God to inspire sin. A god who inspires sin cannot be real. He must be a product of the human mind that has created such a god to legitimize his wrong-doings. Such a god can in no way be a good example for people. God must be the best example of holiness that has no favor and partnership with sin and Satan. His actions, messages and justice must establish people in pure lifestyles and relationships. If a god is not genuine, how could he ask his followers to be genuine?

5. *Why would Allah desire to have the righteous go to hell?*

This is a shocking decree that Allah has settled in the Qur'an (Q.19:66-72). There is a bridge as thin as a single hair that bridges the gap between hell and heaven. Allah places his righteous followers first in hell (Satan's territory) after their death and makes them go through the ordeal of proving to him that they are righteous and can cross over to heaven on this narrow bridge. The purpose of this test, whatever it might be, cannot be attributed to a merciful, holy and just God. What is this test meant to prove? Is this meant to show Allah who is righteous and who is not? If he is all-knowing, does he not already know the righteous from the unrighteous? Also, if Allah really does love the righteous why does he make them pass through hell and experience its bitterness? Isn't this work of Allah in line with the activities of Satan who wishes to have the righteous in hell for any cost? Why does Allah call himself the "God of Mercy" (Q.19:69) despite all the pain he inflicts on man, even the righteous? Why does Allah blame man for their rebellion, if he himself has desired and created man to be rebellious (sinner)? Why would a god, if he is merciful, treat the righteous in the same manner as the unrighteous? Is this the Qur'an's definition of "Mercy"? If the mercy of Allah does not protect a righteous Muslim from the bitterness of hell, what else may be deduced but that this mercy is false?

This is opposite to what Jesus has provided for His followers. He has created a great chasm between hell and heaven as a matter of protection for the righteous (Lk.16:26). Anyone who comes to Christ is clothed in eternal life and the sting of hell is swallowed up in victory on his/her life forever (1Cor.15:53-57; Is.25:8).

6. *What is the difference between the God of the Bible and Allah of the Qur'an?*

According to the Bible, God can in no sense be the author of sin. He created Adam and Eve pure and good, and desired them to use their free choice in obedience to His divine will. However, they were deceived by Satan and were trapped into his evil plans. So, the cause of the original sin that separated man from God is man's wrong decision, not God, whereas the Qur'an attributes the cause of sin to Allah.

Another difference is in the area of salvation. For the God of the Bible, man is disabled by sin and is unable to save himself. Therefore, God saves him. For Allah, man is called to save himself through his own good deeds though he is sinful and has no access to pure goodness. In addition, even though man has tried his best to be righteous in order to gain paradise, Allah does not allow him to go there directly. On his way to paradise, he is first taken to hell (Q.19:68, 71-72). It does not matter whether or not he is a righteous, faithful leader or a prophet; he must be first taken to hell to taste its bitterness.

In conclusion, the Bible states that sin comes from man but not from God. God is Holy and thereby the Savior for the sinner. The Qur'an states that sin comes from Allah into man and man is called to save himself. That is why in Christianity man is certain of his salvation because God is the author of salvation. Through His eternal plan and purpose which He accomplished in Christ, we approach God with freedom and confidence (Eph.3:11-12). But in Islam even the so-called righteous is not certain of his salvation because Allah is the author of sin.

7. *Why would the Qur'an call Jesus the "Word and Spirit of God that became a Perfect and Holy Man" but at the same time deny the Deity of Jesus?*

The Qur'an has borrowed many ideas and beliefs from many sources, including Christian traditions and scriptures that have provided it with a contradictory doctrine. For example, Jesus as the "Word" (Jn.1:1, 14) and the "Spirit" (Lk.1:35) of God is the message of the Gospel that introduces Him as the full revelation of God. It also borrowed from other contemporary Christian ideas that did not believe in the Deity of Christ. These all resulted in a series of contradictory ideas in the Qur'an.

The Qur'an speaks of Jesus on how He came to be a man;

> *We*[15] (God) *sent our spirit to her* (Mary)*, and he* (Jesus) *took before her the form of a perfect man…a holy son* (Q.19:17, 19).
>
> *The Messiah, Jesus, son of Mary, is only an apostle of God, and his* (God's) *Word which he conveyed into Mary, and a Spirit proceeding from himself…*(Q.4:171).

In religious philosophy, God is the "Word" or "Spirit". When someone asks, "What is God?" the answer is the "Word" or "Spirit". Therefore, when God says, "My Spirit", it means "I, God", because, God is the Spirit.

According to the Qur'an, God is Spirit. What, then, does it mean when Allah says in the Qur'an, "We (God) sent our Spirit to Mary, and he took… the form of a perfect man" (Q.19:17), "A Spirit proceeding from God" (Q.4:171)? Is it talking about a creation similar to the creation of Adam when God breathed His Spirit into him (Q.32:8)? No. If it was, then Jesus could not be called "Perfect and

---

[15] In many places in the Qur'an, Allah introduces himself with the plural pronoun "we" which is strange to the doctrine of Islam, which believes Allah is one.

Holy". Like all other men and women, He would also be inspired with sin (Q.91:7-8). However, the Qur'an proves there is not any perfect man in the Qur'an other than Jesus. It is because He is the Spirit of God, unique, Perfect, Holy, Superior to Satan.

According to the Qur'an and Islamic traditions, all humankind, including Muhammad, are from dust, sinners and imperfect creatures, and are in need of salvation. Only Jesus is from God, in and from heaven (Q.4:158, 171), perfect and sinless[16]. As a result, the above Qur'anic verses are the approbations of the Deity of Jesus Christ since they confirm that Jesus is the Spirit and Word of God, and He is Holy and Perfect.

---

[16] Muhammad said, "No child is born but that, Satan touches it when it is born where upon it starts crying loudly because of being touched by Satan, except Mary and her Son." (Dr. Muhammad Muhsin Khan, *Sahih Bukhari Vol.6, Hadith 71*, Published by Islamic University, Al Medina Al Munauwara, P.54, ND.)

God Is Pure in Christianity

Background

Christianity is a monotheistic religion that was based on the redemptive revelation, death and resurrection of Jesus Christ. The Gospel of Jesus Christ teaches that he is the full revelation of God in order to save humankind from the bondage of evil.

The Christian population is the largest population in the world. It has three major divisions; Catholic, Orthodox and Protestant.

Christianity introduces God as a personal and living God without beginning, with absolute stability in truth and holiness (Ps.5:4; Isa.6:3; 1John1:5). God is pure and everything He created was pure. He created humankind and angels with free will. Evil thoughts, words and deeds do not come from God, but from an angel called Satan who has limited power in comparison to God.

Three Persons of the One God

God's mission in the Bible is expressed through the Trinity, the tri-unity of three persons as Father, Son and Holy Spirit. Trinity is not three gods but the three persons of the One God. Because, each person of the Trinity has the full attributes of God's divine nature –just, immutable, omnipotent, omnipresent, omniscient; One is not any greater or inferior than any one of the other two persons of God;

> *The Lord is the Spirit, and where the Spirit of the Lord is, there is freedom* (2Cor.3:17-18).

> *For in Christ all the fullness of the Deity lives in bodily form* (Col.:2:9).

Jesus claimed to be the same as the Father and the Holy Spirit;

> *I and the* ***Father*** *are one. I am God's* ***Son****. Father is in me, and I in the Father. Father or me. All that belongs to the Father is mine. That is why I said the* ***Spirit*** *will take from what is mine and make it known to you* (Jn.10:30, 36, 38; 16:3, 15).

Jesus said that He was with the Father before the world began;

> *Father, glorify me in your presence with the glory I had with you before the world began* (Jn.17:5).

He said that He revealed the Father to His followers;

> *I have revealed you* (Father) *to those whom you gave me out of the world...They know with certainty...All I have is yours, and all you have is mine...We are one* (Jn.17:6, 8, 10, 11,22).

The Christian Trinity cannot be equated with the Hindu trinity, which is the assimilation of three unequal gods; Brahma (the creator), Vishnu (preserver) and Shiva (destroyer). The Christian

Trinity is not an assimilation that originates from other realities but the everlasting Oneness that has perfect harmony in perfect authority, love, will and deed. In a later chapter the Trinity will be discussed, on how it exposes the bondage of sin through the revelation of God and provides freedom out of that bondage. Without meditating on human salvation, the Trinity will be hard to understand.

Questions & Answers

1. *What is the difference between the God of Christianity and the gods of other religions?*

In Christianity God is personal and therefore knowable. We can understand the truth about Him, but in other religions, God is impersonal and unknowable. Putting God in an impersonal position is equal to attributing both good and evil to Him and introducing Him as the source of good and evil. When you research the origin and the beliefs of all other religions, you can understand why their founders attributed both good and evil or light and darkness to God, because impersonality puts God beyond all distinction, including the distinction between holiness and evil, and between light and darkness. If you are not able to know God, you will not be able to say whether or not He is good.

This has caused another doctrinal problem for other religions, including Islam. They have promised their followers a paradise, being with God or being absorbed in Him. It is impossible to believe that people can reach to an impersonal God. An impersonal and unknowable God is also unreachable.

In the same way, it is impossible for an impersonal God to manifest or multiply himself into many inferior beings/gods as many eastern religions believe.

Another difference is in the area of holiness. Except for the God the Bible introduces, all other gods, in one way or another, have a relationship with the evil spirit and people. For example, Muhammad (the prophet of Islam) believed that Allah was with him despite knowing that he was not yet saved or purified. If Allah is a pure and holy god, how can he have a close relationship with people who have not been cleansed from their sins? Another example is that Muslims are called the representatives of Allah on the earth. How can unsaved people, who are not yet transferred from the dominion of sin or, in other words, have not yet entered paradise and therefore have no intimate relationship with Allah, represent him? Adam and Eve, according to the Qur'an, could not have a relationship with Allah ever again because of the one sin they committed. If this is so, how could Muhammad and Muslims represent and have a relationship with Allah on earth? If Allah is pure, then he cannot be represented by any Muslim. In the same way, Muslims cannot represent him. Impurity cannot represent purity. However, all evidence in Islam proves that Allah, unlike the God of the Bible, is linked to sinners and represented by them.

Lastly, in Hinduism, Buddhism, Taoism, and Islam, the gods have caused men and women to suffer by bringing sin and evil into their lives. In Zoroastrianism Satan is infinite like God, and therefore it is impossible for God to overcome the all-powerful him and to bring relief into His followers' lives. As we have discussed earlier, there cannot be two all-powerful beings. This would mean that God and Satan are one and the same in Zoroastrianism.

2. *How does the way of creation vary in the world religions?*

In Christianity, the creation does not exist as a result of God's manifestation or transformation. In fact, manifestation is not creation. The One, Unique and Perfect God cannot transform Himself into multiple inferior creatures as do the gods of eastern religions. The oneness in God cannot be divided or multiplied into incomplete individuals; it cannot be the sum of many individuals either. He is always one and complete and, by His nature, does not have a need for incomplete transformations.

The philosophy of eastern religions brings forth the issue that the conflicts or incompleteness in the nature of god necessitates the creation (a dualistic nature itself is the sign of incompleteness). In other words, god had no choice but to be transformed under the pressure of dualism. This is not the case in Christianity. God is purely good and light. No darkness is found in Him that forces Him into any transformation or creation. He is beyond every reality and in control of everything. Everything exists as the result of His will and love. He is not the source or mother of every creature, but the Creator. He spoke and everything came into existence out of nothing. So, in Christianity, man is not a small part of God, but a person created by God in the image of God.

In Islam, the creation of man is different when compared to Christianity. Allah created the man as the mixture of good and evil (Q. 91:7-8). Whereas in the Bible, the man was created pure, sinless and in the image and likeness of God (Gen. 1:26-27). This reveals a gulf-like gap between Islam and Christianity. In Islam, sin is the product of Allah who is believed to be above everything. Muslims, therefore, have fallen because of Allah and will not be able to rise up if he has desired their fall. Can Muslims resist the will of Allah? However, in Christianity man himself was the cause of his fall, and God desires to lift them up.

What Is Sin and Its Origin?

Hinduism

Sin in Hinduism is ignorance and disobedience to the innate divinity (self-god) that desires spiritual completion. Men and women who stick to the pleasure of the passing world and do not respect the religious traditions and laws are misled and blinded, and are therefore not able to see the truth and reality of Brahman in all forms of life.

In Hinduism sin comes from the ultimate reality or god. God is the cause of good and evil through its manifestations and multiplications. If sin is from god, Hinduism therefore cannot blame man of being blind or irrespective towards truth or traditions.

Buddhism

There is no sin against a divine being in Buddhism. Buddha founded his philosophy on the problem of suffering and on how to get rid of suffering. He believed that the whole of existence is suffering; human nature is fundamentally good; it is the craving and illusion of the body that creates pain and suffering or wages war against every other thing. Deliverance from suffering is attained by following the instructions of Buddha that remove the causes of suffering from the life of a person.

Taoism

In Taoism sin takes place when someone does not live in harmony with the way of nature and upsets the relationship between Yin and Yang. Sin is the product of the female principal of darkness, Yin, originating from Tao (god).

Zoroastrianism

In Zoroastrianism, every evil thought, speech and deed is sin. Sin comes from Satan who is eternal, all-powerful and a rival to the eternal God. Who is able to remove the sin of the all-powerful Satan from human life? This is the major problem that Zoroastrian doctrine is not able to solve.

Islam

All unbelief in Allah, in the Koran and in Muhammad as the apostle of Allah is sin. Avoiding religious obligations (prayer, fasting, etc.), lying, stealing, slandering, etc. are all sin. Although the general belief is that all mankind is born pure, the Qur'an and the Islamic tradition believe that sin was inspired by Allah to humankind (Q.4:88; 7:16-18,179; 9:51; 14:4; 16:93; 35:8; 57:22; 74:31; 91:7-9). This therefore has confused the Islamic scholars in their efforts to construct a sound doctrine for Islam. If sin is from Allah, people therefore are not to be blamed for any sin.

Christianity

Sin in Christianity primarily means the breach of the right relationship with God and alienation from Him (I am my own god now), which is called spiritual death. Sin against God also disrupts our relationship with each other and disintegrates our role in society;

> *Why do you boast of evil, you mighty man? Why do you boast all day long, you who are a disgrace in the eyes of God? Your tongue plots destruction; it is like a sharpened razor, you who practice deceit* (Ps.52:1-2).

> *I have sinned against heaven* (God) *and against you* (man) (Lk.15:21).

In Christianity, the first man and woman sinned against God and departed from Him, falling into Satan's grasp. Satan, unlike God, does not believe in the freedom of choice. He uses all possible options to bind people to himself. That is why he is called "Satan" or "Deceiver". So, in this way, man and woman exposed themselves and their offspring to every evil thought, word and deed and became spiritually lost or dead, unable to save themselves. They became evil-doers and self-centered, incapable of having a genuine relationship with others. They needed a Savior who could release them from Satan, bringing them back to their initial state. Only God could save them.

Unlike all other religions, in Christianity sin does not come from God but from Satan. In Christianity, Satan is not a part of God, whereas he is a part of god in eastern religions. Satan was not made a sinner by God, as is the case with Islam. Instead, he was a good angel, created by God with free will like all other angels, in order to obey the sovereignty of God and be in harmony with His divine love towards all other creatures. However, Satan (Lucifer was his previous name) became proud, desired to be independent of God (to be his own god) and therefore rebelled against the sovereignty of God and His love. His rebellious act caused him to descend from the kingdom of love. The Bible describes his situation as following;

> *How you have fallen from heaven, O morning star, son of the dawn! You have been cast down to the earth you who once laid low the nations! You said in your heart, "I will ascend to heaven; I will raise my throne above the stars of God; I will sit enthroned on the mount of assembly, on the utmost heights of the sacred mountain. I will ascend above the tops of the clouds; I will make myself like the Most High." But you are brought down to the grave, to the depths of the pit* (Isa. 14: 12-15).
>
> *"You were the model of perfection, full of wisdom and perfect beauty. You were in Eden, the garden of God;...You were anointed as a guardian cherub, for so I ordained you...You were blameless in your ways from the day you were created till wickedness found in you...you sinned. So I drove you in disgrace from the mount of God, and I expelled you, O guardian*

> *cherub,...Your heart became proud on account of your beauty, and you corrupted your wisdom because of your splendor. So I threw you to the earth; I made a spectacle of you before kings. By your many sins and dishonest trade you have desecrated your sanctuaries. So I made a fire come out from you, and it consumed you, and I reduced you to ashes on the ground in the sight of all who were watching. All the nations who knew you are appalled at you; you have come to a horrible end and will be no more"* (Ezek. 28: 12-19).

> *He* (Jesus) *replied, "I saw Satan fall like lightning from heaven."* (Luke 10:18).

> *And the angels who did not keep their positions of authority but abandoned their own home – these he has kept in darkness, bound with everlasting chains for judgment on the great Day* (Jude 6).

Then Satan deceived man into rejecting God as all-powerful and all-knowing, and therefore, man followed Satan (Rom. 5:12; 1Cor. 15:21-22). It led man into isolation from God.

So, in Christianity, Satan has his own personal identity and therefore, adversity and sin do not come from God. God is Holy, and in no way can sin be linked to the Holy God. The first man and woman used their choice against God by following

Satan, which led them and their household to a state of godlessness (Gen.3).

A Clear Similarity

Sin seems a big problem in all religions. It has its root in the heart of man right from the very beginning of creation. Every belief gives instructions to its followers to avoid sin and its consequences.

Big Differences

The major differences between Christianity and other world religions are in the following three areas;

1. *The origin of sin:* According to the Bible, sin did not stem from God. However, in other religions, sin stemmed from their supreme beings (gods).

2. *The source of salvation:* In Christianity, man cannot save himself. Only God can save him. Unlike Christianity, all other world religions have asked man, who is sinful and in the bondage of Satan, to save himself. This is impossible. Sinfulness cannot lead to sinlessness. Man cannot be his own savior. Jesus said;

> *"The man who walks in the dark does not know where he is going. Put your trust in the light while you have it, so that you may become sons of light* (Jn.12:35c-36b).

3. *<u>The purity of Jesus:</u>* All divine beings[17], prophets and gurus in other religions are sinful, but Jesus Christ is sinless. He speaks of Himself as the eternal Way, Life, Light, and Truth by whom many may ascend to heaven.

Questions & Answers

1. *According to the world's religions, who is responsible for all injustice in the world?*

In all other religions, except Christianity, gods are the cause of all injustice. All inhumane thoughts and wrong doings have been inspired by gods into man.

2. *Why would people be held responsible for their wrong doings if they were not the major cause of them?*

If gods are the cause of any wrong doing, it would not make sense for people to be held responsible.

3. *Why is the God of the Bible trustful but the gods of other religions not?*

---

[17] In all other religions' scriptures, sin flows down or is inspired from god into man. In other words, this means that "god is a sinner". Because, the inspiration of sin also is a sin in itself.

In all other religions the issue of "good and bad" goes back to the time before creation. The eastern gods had partnership with the devil, and therefore were not immune to evil thoughts and acts. Allah caused Satan to err and made man vulnerable to sin. Gods themselves were not free of evil to stand for good and create a purely good creature. How then could their creatures be free and have free will? That is why they created man and woman in their own likeness, sinners and fallible, without the ability to choose truth or establish themselves in truth. If man is surrendered to Satan he can no longer have freedom. Satan is the enemy of freedom.

In the Bible, sin originated from Satan and penetrated into Adam and Eve. The Bible states that sin cannot have any trace in God's nature. In other words, sin is not eternal as it is in all other world religions. God is eternally pure; in His purity He desired to have pure men and women, free of evil;

> *God did not call us to be impure, but to live a holy life* (1Thes.4:7).

> *The wisdom that comes from heaven is first of all pure; then peace-loving, considerate, submissive, full of mercy and good fruit, impartial and sincere* (James 3:17).

All these say that the God of the Bible is trustworthy.

4. *Why would the God of Christianity create humankind with free will?*

God, in His nature, is free. In accordance with His free nature He desired to give humankind free will. So, the free nature of God is the cause of free will in His creation.

When we talk about the creation of man with free will, it does not mean that this free will can only decide between good and bad. So often we only associate free will with the question "What are we going to choose or follow?" It is first about our identity; "who we are" or "where we stand". This is what leads us to the choices we make (read the next question).
If the genesis of man was devoid of purity and based in dualism, like all other world religions, man would be unable to have free will, since evil is against it. It is for this reason that the right of free will is totally absent in the genesis of man in all other religions. Man claims to have it because it is the desire of their hearts but not the desire of their gods. In other words, their gods are not aware of the cry of their hearts, because they are not real gods.

How can a god create evil if he himself is not evil? If a god is good, why would he create evil for the destruction of his own creatures and kingdom? They, in one way or another, have a connection with evil, which is evident in their thoughts, speech and actions. This being the case, their followers could not stand for the truth. So they cannot say, "We chose to be bad." It was their gods who were bad and created their creatures as evil doers. However, as we have discussed earlier, such gods cannot exist - they are man made gods. Therefore, they are fallible, capricious and lack free will. Only in Christianity is the Creator completely distanced from any evil. He created man in accordance to His holy nature, so that they could have "free will".

5. *Is this free will a sign of God's incapacity to create infallible beings?*

God did not create Adam and Eve (the first man and woman) as fallen or sinful, as other religions state that their gods did. He created them pure and in harmony with His holiness, *for God did not call us to be impure, but to live a holy life* (1Thes. 4:7-8). Also, God did not create them equal to Himself, as all-knowing people, who could know the full depth of His glory, love and grace. Instead, He chose to give them free will with the ability to search and understand and live out these attributes of God. On the other hand, there was no pressure on them to live with God, because they were gifted with the right of "free will". They were placed under His leadership (or fatherhood) and expected to live in harmony with the laws of God's house in order to receive full joy. However, their free will gave them the ability to decide whether or not they wished to be a part of God's kingdom.

The gift of "free will" brought them face to face with a variety of choices. It was to help them see and understand and compare the full value of the life God had placed them in. Options and choices require curiosity, investigation and decision making. It is obvious that there are always temptations involved with different options. Temptation is not sin; it is with man so that he might be able to see the greatness of God's values in comparison with the values of the tempter(s), and therefore allow the Spirit of God to transfer him from his present situation to a higher level. However, if man does not think big and falls short of the sovereignty of God in his confrontation with temptation, he will lose and suffer. The power of temptation is not beyond the capacities of men and women who are united with God and have become part of His family;

> *No temptation has seized you except what is common to man. And God is faithful; he will not let you be tempted beyond what you can bear. But when you are tempted, he will also provide a way out so that you can stand up under it* (1Cor.10:13).

> *He is able to help those who are being tempted* (Heb.2:18b).

So, for God, the main purpose of allowing man to encounter temptation was not that man should cease relationship with Him and be alienated from Him. Instead, it is so that man can understand that God is in control of every thing. Man, thereby, needs to abide in Him with increasing maturity, knowledge, confidence and loyalty, in order to overcome all temptation. So, with God, it is impossible for man to be defeated by temptation.

The gift of "free will" was to allow man to discover the significance of his place in God's kingdom and the extent of God's love towards him. This intimate relationship with God is the source of man's confidence and eternal joy. God has a wonderful hidden message behind every temptation for man to discover through the gifts of his "free will"; searching, thinking and comparing. If we want to put this message in our own words, it might be as follows;

> *I* (God) *had a creative purpose by giving you the gift of "free will". I led you into the realizations of various things and ultimately of my greatness; I am perfect; so, treasure me above all, follow me and rejoice in me.*

So, this is the characteristic of "free will". Man must go through many experiences in order to understand the greatness of God and with open eyes treasure Him above every other thing. He is expected to discover the full scope of God's transformational purpose in His gift of free will in order that he might be victorious over temptation and transformed to a higher glory.

The transformational purpose of God in temptation comes to light in the story of Jesus confronting Satan. The firm standing of Christ against the suggested options of Satan fully illustrates God's expectation of every person's attitude towards temptation. Satan tempted Jesus to eat the bread of his evil mind (Mt.4:3), to throw Himself down from an elevated position (v.6) and to change his citizenship from the kingdom of light into the kingdom of darkness (v.9). As a result of His refusal, Jesus proved that man is to overcome temptation by living with every word that comes from the mouth of God (v.4), by standing in the heavenly and perfect position that God has provided for him (v.7) and by only worshipping the King of kings, the Creator of the universe (v.10). For all those who take their eyes off God and His advice, and aim to live without Him, the confrontation with temptation results in failure. This was why Adam and Eve fell and lost the perfect life God had provided them.

God expected Adam and Eve to glorify His Perfect Standard in all aspects of their lives. He respected their "free-will", however, He did not want their free will to lead them to destruction. Therefore, He warned them of the consequence of any ungodly choices they might have made (Gn.2:17). He never stopped them from facing temptation as it would not be in accord with the essence of man's free will. Rather, He desired to have His presence go with them and become victorious against the ungodly choices.

This is the key for a successful life in God; when God is with you, temptation cannot overcome you instead it becomes a tool making you grow stronger in God. To make a long story short, they made the same mistake Satan did. They relied on their limited self-knowledge and lost.

So, the right to “free will” is not a sign of God’s incapacity to create infallible beings. Instead, it is a sign of God’s full capacity to prove that if man treasures God above all, as Jesus did, he will have a victorious life. The “free will” is to lead man to the full capacity of life with and in God.

Just as a parent desires to have a child, bring him (or her) into life, feed and help him to grow in maturity so does the loving God for His people. There is no parent in the history of mankind who intended to have a child with the intentions of wanting him (or her) to remain an infant forever; unable to learn and unable to walk toward the full capacity of life. There is also no parent who desires to have a child falling against the family values or bringing shame on the family name. If man with his limited ability and love does not have such a desire for his child how could the perfect God with His immeasurable love have such a desire for His people?

Unlike all other gods, God did not create man a sinner or destructor. He created man good and sinless, desired him to obey His perfect values, learn and grow more in His goodness, enjoy life with his Creator and live in peace with others. However, he ignored God and chose to go a different way, choosing a different personality to what God had created in the beginning, a personality that is lost and a stranger to the absolute peace and joy.

Where Is Man Heading?

Is Man Certain of His Salvation?

Can a ‘dualistic god’ save?

Hinduism

In eastern religions, those who do good will become good, and those who do evil will become evil after rebirth. Each soul has many lives. It has no independent identity. Therefore, there is not a Day of Judgment as in Christianity, Islam or Zoroastrianism in which the soul is rewarded or punished once for all eternity. Rather, in Hinduism, each soul is rewarded or punished many times. However, the ultimate hope of a Hindu is a complete release from the Wheel of Rebirth and absorption into the supreme reality. Only the most spiritual Hindus can escape from the Wheel of Rebirth and merge with the absolute.

Unlike Christianity, the hope for promotion to a happier life according to Hindu philosophy lies not in the present life but in the next incarnation. In Christianity, when you believe in Christ you become sure that you are in the kingdom of heaven for all eternity. You know what lies ahead in your future. This is in contrast to Hinduism, where the scenario is quite different. In Hinduism, you do not have a certainty that you will be promoted in the present life. You cannot be certain about your future. All you have is a collection of religious theories that bind you to an uncertain future.

As a result, this uncertainty has become a problem in the Hindu religion. There is no salvation before the next incarnation. There is nothing that can become a light for people regarding their present and future life.

Buddhism

Buddha teaches that every person should meditate on the eroding away of craving and on the dissolution of individuality in order to get rid of suffering and thus gain Nirvana, the state of perfect peace and happiness.

In Buddhism, the cost of a solution for suffering is to reach the complete nothingness of everything, known as 'emptiness'. The notion of emptiness helps a person to release him/herself from any dependency to any person or thing. Since everything is temporary and impermanent, one's existence cannot be absolute but is relative and empty of self-reality. Therefore, if people attach themselves to unreal or empty things (that is, their lives), they will cause themselves suffering, but if they detach themselves from all things, the sufferings will be replaced with happiness and peace.

Buddha left his baby son, his wife and whole family because he believed his partnership with them was the cause of his suffering and therefore a stumbling block towards reaching enlightenment. He wanted to release himself from any attachment to his family in order to gain peace and happiness. However, contrary to his doctrine, Buddha was still keen on maintaining a close relationship with others. This is evident since towards the end of his life he went back to his family and led them to his faith.

It is hard to discover a definition for Nirvana in words, because Buddhists believe in the impermanence of an individual being and reject the existence of a 'soul, self or ego'[18]. If the self is not real, it will also be hard to find a real definition for Nirvana. Buddhists believe that Nirvana is an experience of absorption in peace and happiness that cannot be described in words; it is only an experience. Buddha himself lived it but was not able to describe it; he only described the way of achieving it.

Taoism

In Taoism, salvation is obtained through passivity – taking no action or any moral judgments against good or evil - that opens the way for harmony between two opposite characters in life. With this passive approach, Taoists try to reconcile the dual forces of all life and creation, Yin and Yang, and in this way be at unity with Tao and therefore reach salvation. Contrary to the true meaning of salvation the Taoist salvation is gained through creating harmony between bad and good, but not through overcoming bad with good. From every angle this is a problem.

---

[18] For Buddhists, believing in a human soul is an obstacle to enlightenment, because it produces every kind of selfish desire, which leads to suffering and hinders people attaining enlightenment. However, there are some Buddhists who believe that they have something similar to a soul that enjoys the blessings of the life on earth or goes to paradise.

This is not just a failure in spirituality but also in every aspect of daily life. How can humans survive in a world where the unjust lives side by side with the just? The just will never survive if they are to sit back and allow for injustice to take its course.

Zoroastrianism

Zoroastrianism believes that life is a battleground between good (God) and bad (Satan) and people have to decide to stand for either one of them. It calls upon people to choose the best between the two eternal spirits of good (God) and bad (Satan).

Zoroastrianism says that wise people are those who choose God and follow Zoroaster's instructions of right thoughts, speech, and deeds in order to enter paradise after death in the Day of Judgment, but unwise people follow Satan and enter hell.

However, as discussed earlier, the theory of attributing omnipotence (all-powerfulness) to Satan in Zoroastrianism gives no way for the exercising of free will. Free will is what enables people to choose the best and ultimately salvation. Because God is not above Satan in Zoroastrianism, God is not able to abolish Satan's invasion of people's free will, therefore people will not have access to salvation.

Islam

In Islam, the righteous and unrighteous are firstly taken to hell (Q.19:68-72); then from hell the righteous might go to paradise (heaven) and be with Allah, while the unrighteous stay in hell. However, the ultimate decision belongs to Allah; if he wishes to have unrighteous people in paradise and righteous people in hell, he will do so. Muslims, therefore, are not certain about their future. They believe that they have to try hard to make Allah happy by fulfilling his law in their life on earth. The general belief about the release from the penalty of sin on the Day of Judgment is when a Muslim's good deeds outweigh his/her bad deeds. The Muslims paradise is full of maidens for men (Q.2:25; 44:51-52; 52:17-19).

Christianity

In Christianity, God is the author of salvation. Because of our fallen nature (sinful nature), we are not able to attain purity by our own strength. We need the pure One to take us out of impurity and place us into purity. God is not illogical and does not ask sinners, who are spiritually dead and unable, to save themselves like all other religions do. The only solution for salvation is God. This is also another major difference between Christianity and other religions.

In Christianity, God loves to save sinners and He therefore calls them so He may release them. So if people do not allow God to give them a new life so they may be taken back to their original state into His kingdom, they will remain in the kingdom of death and darkness. After they die, they enter hell for all eternity.

Unsaved people are also not able to reject or give up evil thoughts, words and deeds in their relationships, no matter how much they long to have peace with others, because they are still under the bondage of hatred and hostility. They might be able to use the good part of their dualistic life in order to show friendliness and peace to others, but it will not last long because of the internal opposing forces within them.

However, those who are saved by God are with God and will certainly go to heaven to be with God forever. Those who are not saved cannot be with God and will certainly go to hell.

Christianity believes that human beings live only once on the earth and so have only this chance in their life on earth to be saved. Unlike other world religions, the Gospel of Jesus Christ teaches that salvation only needs to take place once in the present life on earth. In other words, people need to bring God, who is the source of eternal peace and happiness, into their lives on earth. They need to be transferred from the kingdom of darkness into the kingdom of light, which is characterized by the Spirit of love, joy, peace, patience, kindness, goodness, faithfulness, gentleness and self-control while they live on earth. The kingdom of light is not a theory that is aloof from life and its logic; it has values that can be proved in life and by its logic.

The Spirit of light gives birth to a new life on earth and relates that life to the ultimate glory of eternal life in heaven. So in Christianity, the hope of promotion is absolute and has its eternal root in the present life. All traces of needing to depend on Satan have been removed from the life of a person who believes in Christ. Paul, the disciple of Jesus Christ said;

Our citizenship is in heaven (Phil.3:20a).

We, *whose names are in the book of life* (Phil.4:3c), no longer belong to the kingdom of darkness and hell.

Questions & Answers

1. *Why would someone decide to be with God?*

All religious groups commonly believe that man should try his best to get to a position with complete peace and happiness. The cry of the human soul, the crisis amongst the nations and throughout the world all prove that every one desires a place of perfect peace and happiness. All desire to reach God (Ultimate Reality) who is the source of peace, happiness and comfort. No one likes to be hurt by or remain in the claws of evil or evil-doers.

2. *Are all religions heading towards the same goal?*

No!

3. *What is the difference between the savior in Christianity and other religions?*

In Christianity, man has brought sin into his life through Satan and ***God is the Savior***, but in other religions god has created sin and ***man is the savior***. In other religions man has been chained by the so-called all-powerful gods, and then been asked to unchain himself. No man with his limited power is able to abolish the chains of an all-powerful god. That is why the salvation in other religions is uncertain. However, the instruction of Christianity is reasonable; God is pure and therefore can save; the salvation of the pure God is better than the salvation of corrupted man.

Another difference is that in Christianity salvation occurs in this life. Mankind is provided with the opportunity to taste the heavenly life (peace, kindness, love, forgiveness, etc.) in this life. For example, other religions teach people that entry into heaven (paradise or enlightenment) can only occur after death. Christianity, on the contrary, tells us that entry into heaven occurs while we are still on earth.

4. *What is the difference between the ultimate stage of salvation in Christianity and other religions?*

In Christianity man returns to his purest form and has an eternal relationship with the Holy God. However, in other religions, while man is of the opinion that he is heading towards the light, he is instead unconsciously leading himself towards darkness. We have previously discussed that in other religions, gods are the mixture of "good and evil" or the creators of evil. In a dualistic god, the bad is greater than man's. Therefore, if someone aims to reach a dualistic god, he will end up in an unpleasant and impure situation completely opposite to the peace and happiness he was striving to gain.

5. *How would a Hindu describe that he/she has been saved and released from the incarnation and become merged into supreme reality?*

The release or salvation is a very personal matter and is describable only inside the boundary of a person; you are the savior of your own soul and it is for you to know. Hindus say that the experience of release is of such a kind that you become quite certain as to whether it has taken place within you. You not only feel that you have reached the fullness of Brahman but you know it. When you become certain of your release or salvation, you then go and help others to attain salvation.

However, we know that the fullness of Brahman is made up of many gods, good and bad gods. Therefore, salvation cannot be a single individual's experience since many gods exist in the one god as is manifested by that individual. Secondly, a Hindu cannot become certain of his salvation since he was absorbed into the highest form of dualism, Brahman. Dualism is the sign of only impurity and uncertainty.

6. *Is salvation in Hinduism real salvation?*

Not only must real salvation be felt and known by a person, but it must also be felt and known by the whole world as a community. Real salvation has logical and universal values that overcome the boundary of a person in order to peacefully relate him/her to a wider community or world and to the ultimate reality that is in control of the world. Therefore, salvation must be described either by a person who is saved or by a community of individuals who are members of the body of salvation. That is why religions have doctrine in order to raise or arrest the attention of not only an individual but a community of individuals who will build the body of religious communities. As a result, real salvation offers a universal creed that can be tested in the world and not only in the boundary of a person. Secondly, the mergence or absorption of an inferior being into supreme reality is not possible, especially in the case of Hinduism, which believes ultimate reality is impersonal. A personal thing cannot become impersonal and vice versa. Therefore, a Hindu who believes he/she has been released from the incarnation and absorbed into supreme reality cannot be real.

7. *For Buddha, all that exists, including humankind, are unreal and empty of self. If man is unreal and empty, how then does this emptiness break the chain of suffering to reach the fullness of enlightenment? How can emptiness express on one side its release from full suffering and on the other the full joy of peace and happiness in enlightenment?*

The emptiness is meaningless. It is nothing and can reach to nowhere. Dismantling men and women from their souls, hinders them from any promotion towards perfection. A soulless man is like a stone, which does not have any perception of the heat on a sunny day or the chill on a cold day. This might be a reason why the Buddhists claim they are not able to communicate Nirvana, because without a soul even perfect happiness is meaningless.

8. *In what way is Buddha's 'soulless' philosophy irrational and contradictory to his own doctrine?*

The fact that Buddha made an effort to discover a solution to the restlessness of man's soul is clear proof that he was living in contradiction to his selfless theory. After claiming that he received Nirvana, Buddha developed a belief through which people's lives might take on purpose and significance so that their souls could be promoted. He continually used the pronouns 'I' in order to identify his new experience, Nirvana, and 'You' in order to encourage others to reach this stage. These pronouns refer to the existence of Buddha's own 'self' and that of others. The fact that Buddha used 'I' and 'You' is completely at odds to his 'soulless or selfless' doctrine. Secondly, the so-called Nirvana must first reveal itself to the soul in order to create enthusiasm in people for the journey that involves a search, comparison, acceptance and fulfillment. The soul is the immaterial tasting tool of the human being that distinguishes pain from relief. So, the reality or unreality of anything is discovered by the soul through the mind, and tested, compared, evaluated through the heart and chosen through the conscience again with the involvement of the soul. You think with your soul, you decide with your soul, you evaluate with your soul. So in the whole philosophy of life, the soul plays a major role.

9. *Why wouldn't you recommend Zoroastrianism and Islam to people?*

In Zoroastrianism Satan is all-powerful. Therefore, neither God nor man is able to overcome Satan. In Islam, Allah has corrupted man and therefore man is not able to overcome the greatness of this corruption. In addition, Allah takes the righteous (if any) first to hell and then to paradise only if good deeds outweigh their bad deeds. However, the corruption in man caused by Allah and taking the righteous to hell is unjust and illogical.

10. *What would put Christianity above all other religions?*

The scriptures of all major religions, besides Christianity, assert that evil has its origin in God or was created by God. In eastern religions, evil is part of God. In Islam, evil is created by Allah (Q.7:14). Whereas, the Bible states;

> *If the root* (God) *is holy, so are the branches* (God's followers) (Rom.11:16b).

Therefore, an understanding of world religions will certainly encourage people to believe in the pure God of Christianity.

The impurity of a god is frightening and gives people unlimited pain and suffering. Who is foolish enough to have a desire for unlimited suffering? In addition, religions that are the product of impure gods are not real and therefore cannot call upon people to be pure and righteous. How can an unrighteous god call upon people to be righteous? People, who are interested in the truth, never trust unrighteous gods and never desire unlimited pain and suffering.

11. *How would it be possible to distinguish the real God from unreal gods?*

A real God is holy and just, cannot have fellowship with sin, cannot create sin, is against sin and rescues people from sin.

12. *Can man save himself? Can man's good deeds save him?*

Man cannot become his own savior. A prisoner has no authority over the prison to release himself. He is in the bondage of sin and Satan. Only the real God, who is over Satan, can overcome Satan and release man from his bondage.

There is no pure good in anyone's life, which would lead him/her to salvation. If there were pure good in man's life he would no longer need to gain salvation. Man is impure, and impurity cannot lead to perfection.

13. *Which religion offers a pure heaven (paradise) to humankind?*

The concluding section will clearly illustrate why only Christianity offers pure heaven to people.

14. *What is God's plan for the salvation of man?*

After man's fall, God revealed Himself in His fullness (with His full capacity) for saving man and taking him back to his original state of peace and happiness with God.

15. *What does it mean that "God has revealed Himself (entered the world) with His full capacity" in order to save man? What is the motivation behind this revelation?*

God loves the world and does not ignore the cry of man for salvation. For this reason, He has fully revealed Himself and is fully ready to save anyone who desires to be saved.
The Gospel of Christ says;

> *I* (Jesus) *have come that they* (my followers) *have life, and have it to the full* (Jn.10:10b).
>
> *In Christ all the fullness of the Deity lives in bodily form and you* (the follower of Christ) *have been given fullness* (full life or release) *in Christ, who is the head over every power and authority* (Col. 2:9-10).

God is omnipresent. His full capacity is present in His act of creation and in His plan of salvation for man. This is the salvation that the gods in all other religions not only are not able to provide, but also are not expected to provide. As we discussed earlier, they themselves are the cause of man's fall; because of their own dualistic nature they do not have freedom in their own nature and therefore are unable to free man.

A real God, more than a parent, makes Himself fully available, in all dimensions of life, in order not only to save His people (children) but also to make them victorious over the cause of the fall, as Paul, the apostle of Christ said, to make them "more than conquerors";

> *...in all...things we are more than conquerors through him* (God) *who loved us* (Rom.8:37)

God revealed Himself (in Christ) to Paul not only to save him, but also to make him victorious over Satan, destroying Satan's goals and purposes in his heart and mind. That's why he says, we are more than conquerors.

Once we were in the bondage of every bad thought, word and act under the dominion of Satan. We did not have any link to the full strength, love and peace of God. But now, not only are we released from the dominion of Satan but also established on the heavenly grounds, having authority over Satan.

By being established in the love of God, we can drive Satan out of other's lives through the power of love. God not only saved us through His full revelation, but also has built us fully in His power in order to demolish the work of Satan in other's lives. This is why we are called "more than conquerors".

16. *Why do we need the salvation of God for life on earth as well as life after death?*

Salvation on earth means eternal reconciliation with God which leads us to have a peaceful and loving relationship with the nations. When we say that, "We are saved", it means that immoral and unethical values of Satan do not rule our lives anymore. This is what humankind need in their relationships with each other.

Salvation also gives us a freedom which respects other's right to freedom. We live under God's absolute goodness to which nothing can be a threat. We, as a result, do not worry about other ideas or our oppositions and enemies. For us, everybody is free to put his free will to practice. Even Satan is free. We know that by respecting the right of our enemy's free will indirectly praises the absolute goodness of our God. Because, nothing is above His goodness; good is always triumphant over evil. The existence of all other ideas will provide a comparison and reveal the superiority of our freedom and love in Christ.

In conclusion, salvation is the establishment of a right relationship with God and humankind on earth which lasts for eternity.

Ought Not God To Be Just?

Ought Not Man to Encounter God's Justice?

Where Will Man Encounter God's Justice?

The real God is just. He cannot tolerate injustice nor have partnership with it. In His creation, He has created everything, small or big, and put them in an orderly relationship according to His justice. Without justice things could not be combined or related to one another in a nice and peaceful order.

For the Creator a normal and healthy family or society or world is a community in which every member fulfills his or her own role justly in its relationship with others. Without justice, humans live as strangers towards others. It is injustice that has separated people from one another and the truth. It is injustice that has kept people away from knowledge, understanding and friendship and has made them ignorant, unfriendly and hostile towards each other.

God has created humankind in such a way that everybody longs for justice. Even the cruelest person in the world does not like to be treated unjustly. The laws of the nations speak in favor of justice and order people to be just. All religious leaders in the world, in one way or the other, speak in favor of justice. Every person in this world desires justice. God would be inferior to His creation if He were powerless to achieve this. However, He is the most high, holy and just.

If God as the ultimate reality is not just, why should human beings be just or yearn for justice? Why should one not breach the others' rights? If parents are unjust to their children, why should the children be just towards their family and towards society?

Those religions that do not see God as a pure being or attribute evil to Him cannot be called the religions of justice. Evil is against justice. Therefore, if God is just, He cannot have the enemy of justice within Himself. A just God is pure and calls upon every person to be just, or face the consequences.

Where should a man encounter God's justice? In this world, in the world after, or both?

Justice must be applied to every dimension of life. All other religions except Christianity believe that man must face and deal with God's judgment for his actions only after death. They do not believe that people must establish an eternal relationship with God in this life on earth. In other words, they believe that man cannot be purified and justified in this life. However, in Christianity, man can experience God's justice on earth, where evil and temptation take place.

A just God is not satisfied with leaving this world without any justice for three reasons. Firstly, man is instantly accountable for his own wrong doings. Secondly, man needs to have a peaceful relationship with God and others and this requires him to experience superior justice. Thirdly, God does not want man to face the terrible punishment on the Day of Judgment.

A just God does anything that is required to awaken man as soon as possible to experience His justice and so enter His kingdom while on earth. This will help man to have peace in this life and the life after. Likewise, on this earth, we do not postpone justice to the future. For example, when a child does something wrong, the parents do not discipline the child when he becomes an adult, rather, they deal with it at that instant so that the child will not pay severely for the consequences of making that wrong action in the future.

Without the justice of God, life on earth would be terrifying. The only religion that establishes the heavenly court in the hearts of people on earth is Christianity. Man has broken the law in his relationship with God and others, and must therefore encounter the releasing justice of God in this world. The Gospel of Christ says;

> *When you were dead in your sins and in the uncircumcision of your sinful nature,* ***God*** *made you alive with Christ*[19]*. He forgave us all our sins, having canceled the written code, with its regulations, that against us and that stood opposed to us; he took it away, nailing it to the cross. And having* ***disarmed the powers and authorities*** (spiritual forces of evil c.f. Eph.6:12), *he*

[19] Also, read Isaiah chapter 53 (from the OT) on how Jesus was offered unto death as a guilt offering for the sin of the world so that people may be healed in their relationships and have peace with each other.

> ***made a public spectacle of them, triumphing over them by the cross*** (Col.2:13-15).
>
> *The reason* ***the Son of God appeared was to destroy the devil's work*** (1Jn.3:8b).
>
> *It* (the grace of God) *has now been revealed through our Savior, Christ* ***Jesus****, who* ***has destroyed death*** *and has brought life and immortality to light through the gospel* (2Tim.1:10).
>
> ***Salvation has appeared to all men*** (Tit.2:11).
>
> *Christ has set us free* (Gal.5:1).
>
> *We know that we have passed from death to life* (1Jn.3:14).

God's justice saves people from the bondage of sin and lawlessness in life on earth. This is the sign of God's love towards the inhabitants of earth in order to keep their lives measured with the standards of Christ having peace with each other.

Without the Trinity There Is no Salvation

The Trinity (God the Father, the Son and the Holy Spirit) describes God's full revelation and His full purpose for opening human minds and hearts in order that they may understand the cause of sin, its effect in their lives, relationships with each other and God. The Trinity exposes the bondage of sin and provides freedom out of that bondage.

Each person of the Trinity has a mission that indicates to the eternal and unconditional love of God for people to receive peace and freedom. The Trinity proves that God is personal, all-present and accessible so that people can call upon Him to save them.

Paul, the Apostle of Jesus Christ, writes that the ministry of the Holy Spirit is to inspire a lasting righteousness into men and women's hearts and to give them life (2Cor. 3: 8-10, 6c). He calls these men and women "*a letter from Christ,..., written not with ink but with* ***the Spirit of the living God****, not on tablets of stone but on tablets of human hearts*" (v.3); a letter of freedom from Christ for the world or *the aroma of Christ that spreads everywhere the knowledge of God* (2Cor. 2: 14-15). Paul writes that Christ has paid the price for freedom, redeemed Christians from the lord of evil, Satan, and removed the veils that once covered their minds and hearts so that they can have knowledge of God, reconcile with Him, receive His righteousness and freedom, and also minister to others to receive that freedom (read 2Cor. 5: 17-21). He says, "*Whenever anyone turns to* ***the Lord***

(Christ), *the veil is taken away. Now* ***the Lord is Spirit****, and where the Spirit of the Lord is, there is freedom* (2Cor. 3: 17). *"...by him* (the Spirit) *we cry, "Abba, Father." The Spirit himself testifies with our spirit that we are God's children"* (Rom. 8: 15-16; Gal. 4: 6). In his letter to the Corinthians, Paul writes that God calls those people, who distinguish the difference between God and idols and are not yoked together with idol worshipers, His sons and daughters (2Cor. 6: 14-18).

The verses above are only a few of the many verses in the Bible which prove either *God or Jesus is the Spirit and the same.* There is no difference in their essence but only in their mission. In essence, He is one and unique. He is called Father, Son, or the Holy Spirit only because of His various missions towards humankind;

> *There is ...one Spirit...one Lord; one God and Father of all* (Eph. 4: 4-6).

The presence of the Trinity challenges the minds, hearts and consciences of people so they may get rid of any lawlessness or unrighteousness in their lives. He (Trinity) establishes a 'spiritual court' in people's hearts, reveals Himself as the full example of righteousness, holiness and justice, challenging them to get rid of Satan, the source of lawlessness. So the Trinity makes salvation accessible in life on earth, contrary to the world religions that introduce salvation as an impractical theory inaccessible in this life.

Jesus said;

> *Now is the time for judgment on this world; now the prince of this world will be driven out...I have come into the world as a light, so that no one who believes in me should stay in darkness* (Jn.12:31, 46).

Those religions that leave the salvation of man for life after death are, consciously or unconsciously, rejecting the fulfillment of God's justice on earth and in this way supporting the spread of immorality. Man, to get rid of immorality and unrighteousness, needs the full revelation of God's absolute justice and truth in all dimensions of his life on earth. This unchains him from the dominion of Satan, purifies his thoughts, words or deeds and enables him to walk with God in righteousness.

So the triune revelation of One God is to abolish the work of the lawless Satan in the life of people, release and bring them into an intimate relationship with Him. This freedom happens in the heart and man can experience God's justice in the heart, where evil and temptation take place. That is why man must allow his heart to be the place of the 'spiritual court' for the revelation of God's justice, holiness and love.

Who is qualified to sit on the throne of justice in this spiritual court in the heart of man; God, man himself or Satan? Is any man or woman qualified to be the judge of this court? Has any person in the world (including prophets) ever obeyed God to absolute perfection and is absolutely moral, wise enough and capable enough to defend the case for God? No! As the book of Job says;

> *Will you* (as betrayer) *argue the case for God? Can he who hates justice govern?* (Job 13:8b; 34:17b).

Sin or immorality or unrighteousness is a problem in everybody's life. Man is in the bondage of unrighteousness and cannot stand for God who is absolutely moral and righteous. Secondly, he is guilty of cooperating with Satan. Thirdly, he needs a more powerful force to unchain him. Last but certainly not least, the imperfect man is not able to defend God's perfect law of justice. For these reasons, it is above and beyond the capacity of man to undertake the task of judgment and save himself.

This is why as Christians we believe that men and women cannot save themselves. Before receiving salvation, no one is able to obey and fulfill the perfect law of God. Because of imperfection mankind is unable to save himself. As a result, religions that call their people to act and be righteous before salvation are irrational and untrue.

Who else except God can take over the judging role in that court? Not one creature less than God is able to do so. **It is only God who is able to establish the court and be the judge over it.**

Why would God, whose laws were breached by man, be interested in establishing such justice in this world in order to rescue man? The only reason that the Bible gives is the love of God towards humankind. He has created humankind for Himself and loves them. **So, God's love along with His justice is another motivation behind His will to rescue man and remove the lawlessness from his heart.**

One reason that God is called 'Father' in the Bible is because through His Mighty love and justice He can renew the life of people and make them brothers and sisters to each other, the members of one body, family and kingdom. So the Spirit of Fatherhood takes the responsibility to rescue people from the bondage of Satan, the prince of lawlessness, and restore them into His Kingdom.

Can man be released without paying the cost for his sins? A just religion cannot release a sinful man without covering the cost of his sin. Because man had a free will, and with this free will chose to break God's law, he now has to pay the cost. Justice cannot ignore the cost of lawlessness.

Again the question rises here; can man cover the cost of his sins and save himself? The response is 'no'. Is there any one who can pay the cost for man and rescue him? Using the same logic as above, God is the only source that can pay the cost for man and release him.

What motivates God to pay the penalty for man? It is His love towards man. The Bible says that man cannot pay the cost or save himself, because he is spiritually dead. Can a dead person bring himself back to life? The answer is 'no'. Who then is able to bring man back to life? God, God, God! Since man cannot reach God the only solution is for God to reach out to man. God entered this lawless world (the world of death), paid the price on the Cross, breaking down the barrier between man and Himself, making the spiritual resurrection from death to life possible. He revealed Himself as the Son and redeemed man announcing victory over death. In other words, one of the three persons of God, the Son Jesus, was incarnated for the purpose of giving His life as a ransom for sinners so that they may be released and approach God with freedom and confidence.

In the beginning, man was with God; however, Satan deceived him to misuse his freedom, drew him out of the kingdom of God and placed him into the kingdom of death. But this time, God as Son entered the kingdom of death and brought man back into His kingdom, to be with Him. While Satan killed man spiritually, Jesus brought him back to life spiritually. While Satan made man lawless, Jesus brought him back into lawfulness. While Satan removed the loving attitudes from his heart and mind and inspired him with hatred, hostility and bloodshed, Jesus took him back to His kingdom and dressed him with love. This loving and just approach is only possible by the God of the Bible. Because, He is Holy!

God's Holiness (Holy Spirit) is the third person that is revealed in the Trinity. The Holiness of God is a tool He uses to implant His love and justice into man's heart. In other words, God not only calls people to be holy, but also regenerates them in His holiness enabling them to live a totally new life. Man cannot be holy unless he is transferred from the dominion of sin into the dominion of righteousness. Contrary to the teachings of other religions, sin, in Christianity is not a wrong doing but a wrong being that leads to wrong doing. Therefore, it is firstly man's identity, not actions that have to be changed. If they are not rescued from the dominion of Satan, they will not be able to do good. However, when God's holiness is implanted into their hearts, they are convicted of their ungodliness, and led to accept His justice and the ransom He paid for their release. This is the sovereign work and call of God through His triune personalities. In other words, the Trinity first changes the identity into righteousness and then calls them to act righteous.

Not only did God love man and pay the penalty for his transgressions, releasing him from the bondage of Satan, but He also resided in the life of man as the Holy Guardian, Teacher, Leader, Protector, Speaker and Sanctifier in order to sustain man with love, joy, peace, patience, kindness, goodness, faithfulness, gentleness and self-control (Gal. 5:22). As Paul, the disciple of Christ, said;

> *For God did not call us to be impure, but to live a holy life. Therefore, he who rejects this instruction does not reject man but God, who gives you his Holy Spirit* (1Thes. 4:7-8).
>
> *God chose you to be saved through the sanctifying work of the Spirit and through belief in the truth. He called you to this through our gospel, that you might share in the glory of our Lord Jesus Christ...May our Lord Jesus Christ himself and God our Father , who loved us and by his grace gave us eternal encouragement and good hope, encourage your hearts and strengthen you in every good deed and word* (2Thes. 2: 13b-14, 16-17).

Therefore, the God of universe revealed His intimate triune personalities in order to release man and give him new life. In biblical terminology, God is called; Father, Son and the Holy Spirit and all is One and eternal (Deut. 32:6; 33:27; Ps. 2:7; John 1:1; 10:30; Rom. 9:5b; 2Cor. 3:14-18; Eph. 4:6; Titus 2:13; Heb. 1:8; 9:14; 13:8; 2Peter 1:1; Rev. 1:18);

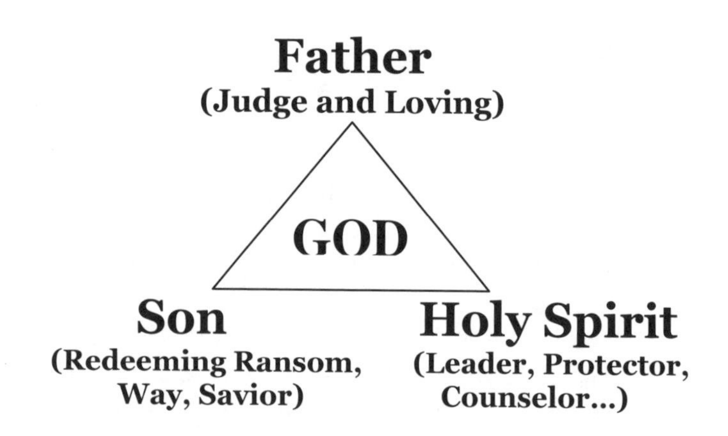

It is through the Revelation of God's triune persons, who are one in essence, that man can be released and enlivened in all dimensions of his life;

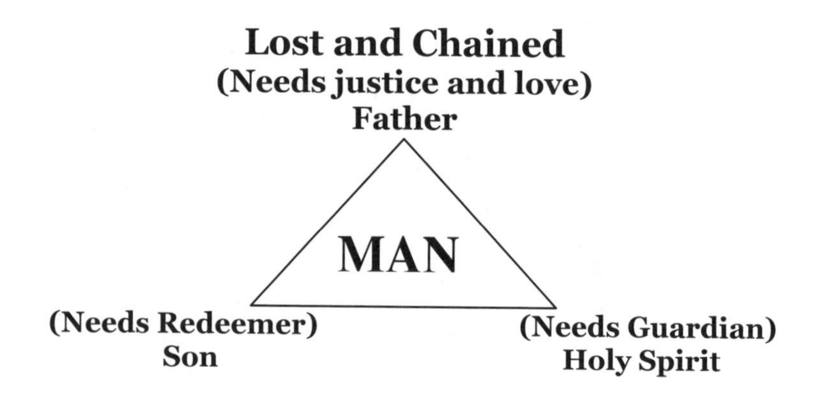

Man is lost and chained and in need of a redeemer and guardian. A lost person needs a loving guardian, someone who intimately and tirelessly pays the cost to release him and give him further help and shelter. Someone who loves, nurtures, guides, encourages, teaches and does everything within his power to equip his child for life. If a parent would use all his abilities, attributes and wealth to find his lost and troubled child, how much more would God, in all His being, labour for the one whom He loves and has created for Himself?

Who can be the good, caring guardian other than the mighty God, who is the source of unconditional love? Who can, other than God, give eternal assurance and confidence to a lost man? When can a lost man take shelter in God and call Him Father? The answer is, "Only when God reveals Himself fully and personally".

The full revelation of God to save man is only comprehensible through the Trinity. The following words of Christ clearly illustrate the above;

> *A slave has no permanent place in the family, but a son belongs to it forever* (Jn.8:35).
>
> *I will not leave you orphans; I will come to you. I will send to you the Spirit of truth who goes out from the Father, whom the Father will send in my name. Peace I leave with you; my peace I give you. If anyone loves*

> *me, he will obey my teaching. My Father will love him, and we will come to him and make our home with him* (Jn.14:18; 15:26; 14:26, 23, 27).

Jesus said to His followers that He would not leave them orphans or fatherless. His words bring forth the meaning that He will be coming daily to His followers in His Triune personalities (Father, Son and Holy Spirit), will visit them through His grace and in this way leave them with peace.

Without the Trinity, life is dangerous and hostile. Jesus made clear in His words the reason for the hostility of those Jews who aimed to kill Him. It was because they were not the children of God; they were Fatherless. If they belonged to God, they would fear God's justice and doubtlessly love Jesus. Jesus said to them;

> *You are determined to kill me...If God* (*the judge*, v.50) *was your Father, you would love me...but...you dishonor me* (Jn.8:40, 42, 49).

So, the Message of Christ is to challenge and open the minds of people in order to understand that God is personal and that His Triune[20] personalities are

---

[20] Just as a parent can be called loving towards his child, a redeemer and helper, so is God as Father (lover), Son (redeemer) and Holy Spirit (helper). Tri-unity can be discovered in many things and places. Water is ice, liquid and steam; time is future, present and past; man is father, son and husband; woman is mother, daughter and

of vital importance for transferring people from hostility into caring, loving and peaceful attitudes (fatherliness).

The revelation of Jesus Christ is not like the natural birth of humankind that is evolved out of the human race or made of dust as in the case of Adam. In His revelation, God comes from Above, becomes Man in His absolute perfection and enters into human history. He, therefore, is not from this world and cannot be equated (as in the case of Islam and other religions) with any who are of this world, since we are all made of dust and once dead, return again to dust. Unlike the man of this world, Jesus is from and in heaven, and in control of everything.

Questions & Answers

1. *Why is God called "The Son" in His redeeming mission? Couldn't He simply be called God in all His missions for mankind?*

The Bible uses the word "Son" to describe God as a **personal** God who can **reveal** Himself in all dimensions of human life in order to redeem them fully for reconciliation;

---

wife. Every person is soul, spirit and body (1Thes. 3:23). Each personality manifests itself for the particular position and role, but they are all one in essence and united in one person or thing.

> *He* (Jesus) *is the image of the invisible God, the firstborn over all creation. For by him all things were created in heaven and on earth, visible or invisible,...for him. He is before all things, and in him all things hold together...For God was pleased to have **all his fullness dwell in him**, and through him to reconcile to himself all things, whether things on earth or things in heaven, by making peace through his blood, shed on the cross* (Col.15-20).

This is not a cleverly invented theory like all other religions that have stemmed out of human minds, holding celebrations in honor of man-made gods and collecting adherents for what is not real (Acts 7:41). Jesus (the Son) has given many proofs about His equality with God (the Father), by doing the unique works of God (Matt.5:43-48; Jn.5:21-30; 6:40; 11:38-39, 43-44; Acts 1:3). He said; "*I* (Jesus) *am God's Son." "I and the Father are one." "Whatever God does the Son also does*". "*He gives eternal life*" (Jn.10: 30, 36c-38; 5:19; 17:2). His disciples, who lived with Him and saw Him after the resurrection, all approved His equality with God. Peter said;

> *We did not follow cleverly invented stories when we told you about the power and coming of our Lord Jesus Christ, but we were eye-witnesses of his majesty. For he received honor and glory from the Father when the voice came to him from the*

> *Majestic Glory, saying, "This is my Son, whom I love; with him I am well pleased." We ourselves heard this voice that came from heaven when we were with him on the sacred mountain* (2Pt.1:16-18).

Paul, who once was one of the persecutors of the early church because of her belief in Jesus as God, saw the risen Jesus (1Cor.15:8-9). This encounter completely convinced him that Jesus and Father were one and the same Creator of all things;

> *"The Father from whom all things came and for whom we live; and* the *Lord Jesus Christ, through whom all things came and through whom we live* (1Cor.8:6; read Col.1:15-17).

What Do We Need to Follow?

Conscience: Capable of Seeing the Truth

Do you believe that God is Holy? If your answer is "yes", then this is "yes" to Christianity and "no" to all other religions, since it is only in Christianity that God is holy. In eastern religions, the devil is in god's own nature, and in Islam, it is Allah who has corrupted Satan and inspired sin in man.

Do you believe that God must be the source of all certainty? If your response is "yes", then it is "yes" to Christianity and "no" to all other religions, because the dualistic nature of gods in other religions has made them unable to give assurance to their followers. If you ask a follower of Christ, "Are you saved?" The response will be, "Yes, of course", whereas in all other religions, no one is certain of his/her present and future spiritual position.

Do you have a holy relationship with the real God? Do you want to have fellowship with God and be with Him from now until eternity? Do you want to be His salt and light among the nations of the world and stand for His absolute peace, love and justice? If your response is "yes", therefore, it is necessary for you to search first for the real God, understand Him and then commit yourself to Him and get into such living relationship with Him as His salt and light.

Your conscience is the only part of your life which is completely capable of seeing the truth. Listen to your conscience, distinguish the truth from the false by reflecting on these concluding words and decide which path you need to follow.

The Nature of Gods Compared

The nature of the Supreme Realities and their relationship with Satan (or spiritual enemy) in different religions can be summarized as follows.

In Hinduism, Mahayana Buddhism, Taoism and Zoroastrianism, gods cannot be called holy. In one way or another, they are the creators of sin and spiritual darkness. This shows that darkness is in their essence. An impure god cannot be a real God but a man-made image, the mixture of light and darkness. How can such a god be trusted? In fact, a god with this characteristic cannot exist.

People are taught to cherish desires in their hearts and meditate on these gods in order to be absorbed in or join them. However, people are not aware that their own spiritual position is better than their gods. If we show a Hindu's spiritual being with this sign ◑ and Brahman with the larger circle below, we will be able to understand why a shift from the position of human to god is both dangerous and irrational. Man, as a little manifestation of a great god, has a fairly small amount of darkness compared to god. In light of this comparison, why would someone wish to have a shift from a relatively bad position to an extremely worse state?

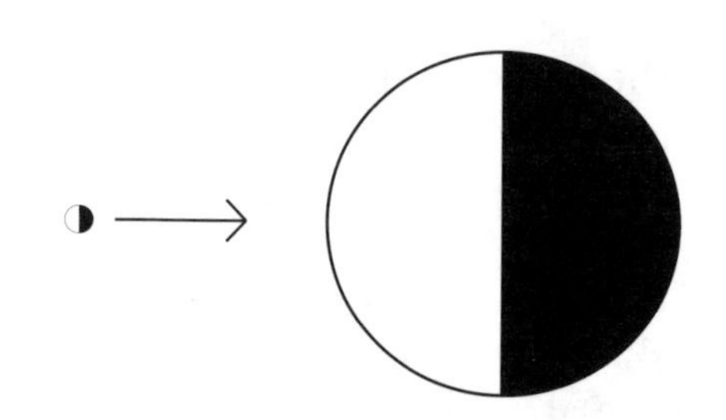

Hindu God
(The Source of Impurity)

In Theravada Buddhism god and everything else is the creation of the mind and nothing is real. If this is the case, Buddha's advice cannot be real as it is the product of his own mind. It contains much uncertainty and confusion.

God in Buddhism
(Product of Mind)

In Islam, though Allah is called holy and pure, he is described as the inspirer of sin to Satan and man. This dualistic doctrine does not present Allah as just and holy. How can the Holy God desire man to be a sinner? If Allah has made man a sinner and unrighteous, then he cannot call upon man to be righteous. However, as previously mentioned, purity cannot inspire impurity. It is impurity that begets impurity.

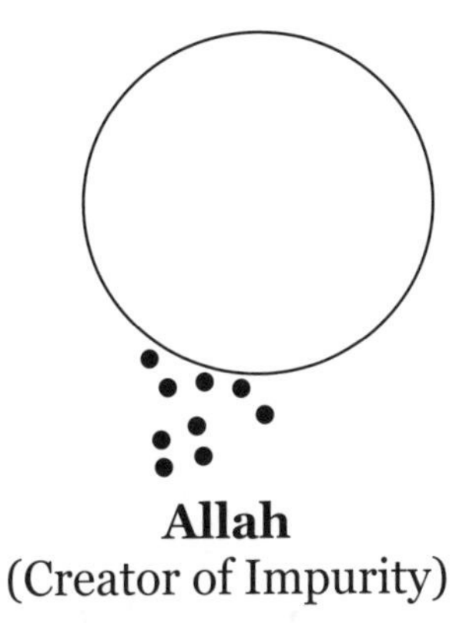

Allah
(Creator of Impurity)

In Christianity, God is holy and pure. In the beginning, His creation resembled His nature. He cannot create sin nor have partnership with sin or sinners. Sin entered into man's life through Satan, separating him from God. Man is in need of a Savior as he is unable to save himself from the dominion of Satan. God, as the source of all purity, provides a clear path for man that leads to salvation.

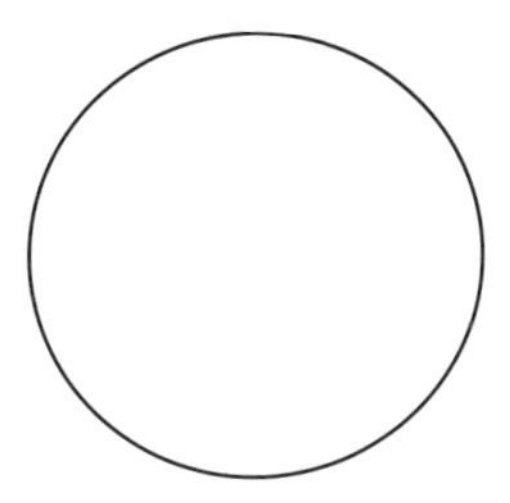

Pure God (Jesus)
(The Absolute Source of Purity)

The Heavens Compared

In Christianity, man has to be completely purified in order to enter heaven. If we illustrate man as a rectangle and heaven as a circle, heaven in Christianity can be portrayed as follows;

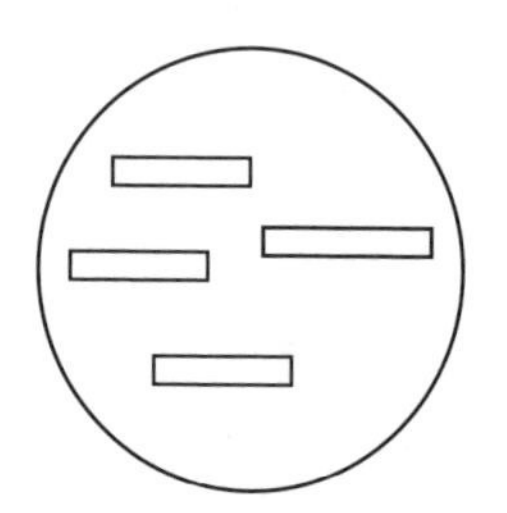

Heaven with Purity

In other religions heaven is not immune of sin. For example, Islam believes that if the righteousness of a man outweighs his unrighteousness he will then enter heaven. Therefore, it is unnecessary for the complete purification of man as illustrated below;

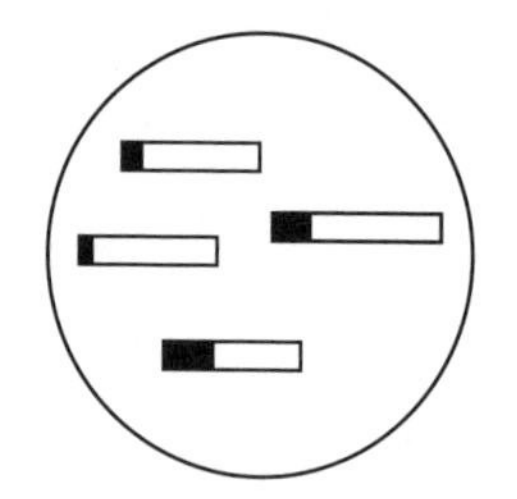

Heaven with Impurity

The above diagram shows that darkness (sin) has entered paradise (heaven) through man. There is no paradise with black dots of hell in it. Such a paradise does not match the holiness of God. However, we know that darkness can in no way have access to a pure heaven. A heaven with impurity cannot be real. Heaven, by definition, is the place of absolute purity and perfection. It is the dwelling place of the Holy God. It is the place for those who have allowed the Holy God to completely drive Satan out from their lives and release them from his dominion.

Why then does Allah allow Muslims, who are not purified and do not believe in complete purification, to enter paradise (heaven) and have partnership with him? If Allah is pure, how can he have partnership with the unpurified?

The answer is obvious. Allah is not pure, hence his partnership with sin.

How is Good and Bad Weighed?

How can it be that other religions compare good and bad in order to see which outweighs the other? What good acts can outweigh bad acts such as murder or rape? Can giving your wealth to charity remove the effect of your crime on victims or their families?

By breaking a human heart, you have also broken God's heart, as He created humankind for Himself and loves them with His whole being. You cannot win God's heart with your so-called good deeds unless you allow God to renew you so that you are no longer a threat to society. It is only through God that this transformation is possible. This, in turn, delivers you from all self-centeredness, destroying the transgressions of the mind and heart, releasing you from their bondage. This supernatural transformation reveals the absolute justice, love, and purity of God and renews you completely in all dimensions of life. It instills the love of God into your heart, creating a faith that says without the absolute love of God you are nothing, thus expelling the whole notion of weighing good and bad. As Paul, the disciple of Christ, says, ***"When perfection comes, the imperfect disappears"***. Or to put it in other words, "When good (Christ) comes, bad (Satan) disappears";

> *If I speak in the tongues of men and of angels, but have not love, I am only a resounding gong or a clanging cymbal. If I have gift of prophecy and can fathom all mysteries and all knowledge, and if I have a faith that can move mountains, but have not love, I am nothing. If I give all I possess to the poor and surrender my body to the flames, but have not love, I gain nothing. Love is patient, love is kind. It does not envy, it does not boast, it is not proud. It is not rude, it is not self-seeking, it is not easily angered, it keeps not record of wrongs. Love does not delight in evil but rejoices with the truth. It always protects, always trusts, always hopes, always perseveres. Love never fails. But where there are prophecies,*

> *they will cease; where there are tongues, they will be stilled; where there is knowledge, it will pass away. For we know in part and we prophesy in part, but **when perfection comes, the imperfect disappears*** (1Cor. 13:1-10).

The Gospel of Christ rejects the theories of salvation in all other religions, which hold the notion that unpurified and unperfected man can enter the perfect heaven or paradise. Therefore, in all other religions, heaven is left with an unsolved problem of sin. As evident in the previous diagram, man in other religions, though with a "heavy balance", is not completely cut off from his relationship with Satan even after entering heaven. On the contrary, in Christ, a man must be completely purified and cut off from his relationship with Satan prior to entering heaven. In no way can a trace of darkness be found in Christ's heaven. This proves that salvation and freedom in Christ is absolute whereas in other world religions it is relative and therefore uncertain.

The Salt and Light of the World

A purified person, the person whose relationship with Satan is completely annulled, can play a significant role and become a good spiritual, moral and ethical example of truthful living among others. A person with such characteristics is only found among the followers of Christ.

The Gospel of Jesus Christ writes that peace and love come from a pure heart and a good conscience and a sincere faith that encourages understanding and affirms confidence (1Tim.1: 3-7). It maintains that the church of Christ can make the manifold wisdom of God known to the nations of the world (Eph. 3: 7-10).

Why would the followers of Christ be chosen for such a great task? The followers of Christ, unlike the followers of all other religions, have a pure God and Savior, a pure heaven, a purified life and a certain and perfect salvation in order to become a good example for life among all nations. In Christianity, life is centred on and led by purity, whereas in other religions impurity is the source of life. Gods in other religions are impure in their nature, so too are their paradises. They have asked their followers to rely on their own impure human strength in order to reach to purity. But the fact remains that impurity cannot and does not lead to purity.

The Bible provides some unique characteristics of Christians that set them apart as the salt and light of the world:

1. The church (the followers of Christ) is purified of sin, unchained from the dominion of Satan and has approached God with freedom and confidence through faith in Jesus Christ (Eph. 3: 11-12). So the followers of Christ have been clothed in real freedom and can represent it among others.

2. The wisdom that has been given to the church comes from God and it is pure, peace-loving, considerate, submissive, full of mercy and sincerity. Peacemakers who sow in peace raise a harvest of righteousness (James 3: 17-18). So the followers of Christ have received their peace-loving wisdom from God - the source of absolute love. Through Christ, they have been reconciled to God, transferred from the kingdom of hostility into God's peace-loving kingdom. As they are the children of peace they can have peace with other nations and can call the world to reconcile to God and to each other (Col. 1:20; 2Cor. 5:17-21).

3. The church is rooted and established in the love of Christ and therefore derives its name from the Holy God (Eph. 3: 15, 17). It has tasted God's righteousness and kissed His peace (Ps. 85: 10). The followers of Christ, unlike all other religious groups, are not established by human strength. They are, instead, established in the holiness of God whose love is absolute and unconditional.

For these reasons, the Bible calls the followers of Christ the salt and light of God for the world (Matt. 5:13-14); the salt that cleanses hearts from false values, beliefs and behaviors in order to preserve a good and righteous relationship with others; and the light that unveils the destructing values of other beliefs in order to lead hearts and minds to the source of absolute love, justice and holiness.

Isn't it beautiful to be clothed with these characteristics? The key is "understanding". The knowledge of God produces a sincere heart with full assurance that leads people to the Light and to a life of peace with one another.

Bibliography and Resources for Further Study

Cavendish, Richard, *The Great Religions*, London: Contact, 1980.

Eberhard, Wolfram, *A History of China,* London: Routledge & Kegan Paul Ltd. Pub., 1967.

Fairbank, John K. and Goldman, Merle, *CHINA A New History,* USA: The Belknap Press of Harvard University Press, 1998.

Halverson, Dean C. (General Editor), *World Religions,* Minneapolis, Minnesota: Bethany House Pub., 1996.

Heydt, Henry J., *A Comparison of World Religions*, USA: CLC, 1976.

Langley, Myrtle, *Religions*, England: Lion Pub., 1981.

Lochhaas, Philip H., *The Eastern Religions,* USA, Missouri: Concordia Pub., 1970.

Mass, Nuri, *Many Paths One Heaven,* Australia, NSW: The Writers' Press, 1965.

Muhsin Khan, M. *Sahih Bukhari Vol.6, Hadith 71*, Published by Islamic University, Al Medina Al Munauwara, P.54, ND.)

Sahih Al-Musim *Hadith* No.1277 & 1278.

Savage, Katharine, *The History of World Religions*, London: The Bodley Head, 1970.

Schirokauer, Conrad, *A Brief History of Chinese and Japanese Civilizations,* USA: Harcourt Brace Jovanovich, Inc., 1978.

Schlink, M. Basilea, *Christians and TM Yoga?*, Australia: Evangelical Sisterhood of Mary, 1975.

Sherratt, B.W. and Hawkin, D. J., *GODS AND MEN*, London: Blackie, 1972.

Stewart, Dicks & Mennil, Paul & Santor, Donald, *The Many Faces of Religion,* Canada: Ginn and Company, 1973.

Yamamoto, J. Isamu, *Buddhism, Taoism & Other Far Eastern Religions,* Michigan: Zondervan Pub., 1998.

Yamamoto, J. Isamu, *Hinduism, TM &Hare Krishna,* Michigan: Zondervan Pub., 1998.

http://www.comparativereligion.com/man.html, *The Ultimate Reality in World Religions*, 2002.

http://www.comparativereligion.com/evil.html, *The Problem of Evil in World Religions,* 2002.

http://www.comparativereligion.com/avatars.html, *The Divine Incarnation in Hinduism and Christianity.*

http://www.catholiceducation.org/articles/apologetics/ap0008.html,*Comparing, Comparing Christianity and Hinduism.*

http://sino-sv3.sino.uni-heidelberg.de/FULLTEXT/JR-EPT/william1.htm, *Endo and Johnston talk of Buddhism and Christianity. (Novelist Shusaku Endo, Jesuit theologian William Johnston) (Interview)*

Bible, NIV

Koran

Avesta